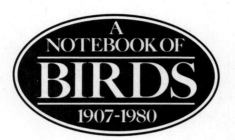

Robert Gillmor

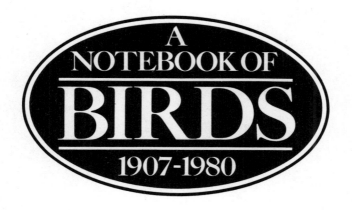

A NOTEBOOK OF BIRDS 1907-1980

with a commentary by
Jim Flegg

and illustrations by
Norman Arlott, Robert Gillmor and Laurel Tucker

M

First published 1981 by
Macmillan London Limited
London and Basingstoke

Associated companies in Auckland, Dallas,
Delhi, Dublin, Hong Kong, Johannesburg,
Lagos, Manzini, Melbourne, Nairobi,
New York, Singapore, Tokyo, Washington
and Zaria

British Library Cataloguing in Publication Data

Flegg, Jim
   A notebook of birds 1907–1980
   1.Birds
   I.Title
   598   QL673

   ISBN 0-333-30880-8

Phototypeset in Great Britain by
Filmtype Services Limited, Scarborough.

Printed in Great Britain by
Butler & Tanner Ltd, Frome and London.

Contents

To Matthew and William

Acknowledgements

Tim Sharrock and Julian Ashby hatched the idea of this book, and Robert Updegraff was inevitably practical and helpful during its design and production. Martin Woodcock, the lucky possessor of a full set of *British Birds*, generously allowed me free range amongst them. Robert Gillmor, Norman Arlott and Laurel Tucker have pierced the sombre banks of text with shafts of their artistic sunlight, for which I am most grateful.

All bird watchers – at least all married bird watchers – owe special gratitude to their wives for their tolerance of a hobby with such antisocial habits and hours. Caroline, my wife, also has to put up with my writing schedule – on this occasion typing the manuscript very much at arm's length, finishing at hectic pace the evening before our second son William was born. The word 'thanks' is far from adequate.

Introduction

British Birds is a monthly journal, first published in 1907. From its inception, it has contained a palatable blend of full papers on bird biology, behaviour, ecology and identification and shorter 'Notes' and 'Letters', designed to allow the permanent and proper documentation of the 'one-off' observation or record. These notes differ only in dimension – length, breadth or depth – from the longer papers. The factual material they contain, and some of the arguments or debating points of view that they put forward, lack nothing in substance, merit or (especially) interest.

This book is one bird watcher's anthology of seventy-three years of notes from the journal. The task of selecting suitable material was daunting, and far more arduous than ever I anticipated: several sister volumes could be compiled from the residue of this one! The saving grace was the absorbing interest of the whole operation: I had to read just about every note and was unable to skip any pages. In much the same way as the search of a dictionary for a particular word is often side-tracked by its neighbours, so were my attempts at a logical approach thwarted by the fascination of each paragraph. But the job is done; as a selection, undoubtedly some of my own interests and biases must show through, but I take comfort from the fact that an anthology *is* essentially personal. I have tried to squeeze in as much material as the number of pages – the final arbiter – would allow, and to keep my choice as wide as possible without producing a compendium of disconnected jottings. In making my selection, I was governed by topic, and not by author. Omission casts no slur, and any recorder feeling affronted has my apologies, but can take comfort that he is in the company of famous men, past and present!

Our thanks are due to those bird watchers who have not only seen, but studied; who have not just watched, but who have recorded what they have seen for us all. Without them, this book would not have been possible. There is an old saying, dating from the days when much of ornithology centred on birds shot specially for study: What's hit is history, what's missed is mystery. This has a wider truth, and a wider applicability than just to the obtaining of specimen corpses. Where would we be, not solely in our knowledge and understanding of birds, but in our enjoyment of them, without the bird watchers who take the trouble to place on record what they have seen? These pages should serve to indicate that the passage of time, and inevitable natural (or unnatural) change, will always ensure a plentiful supply of fresh topics for the ready observer.

⇥ 1 ⇤
Behaviour

Bird behaviour is a vast topic: just about every note ever published in *British Birds* could, in some way, be catalogued under this heading. Consequently, this chapter contains a selection of notes relating to only a few topics, but many, many others will be found elsewhere in these pages.

Most of us have seen the sitting birds in a gullery, or a feeding flock of waders or Starlings, suddenly rise as one bird and wheel about the sky, calling. Besides marvelling at the visual acuity and muscular co-ordination that make such mass evolutions possible, most of us have probably assumed that such alarms and excursions serve to protect the birds: if one bird moves, the others do, just in case there is real danger.

'Alarms', 'dreads' and 'panics' at terneries   It is a well-known phenomenon for an entire colony of terns *Sterna* suddenly and for no accountable reason to take flight in alarm with much noise and then, after a short period, to return to normal. Apart from possible disturbance by man or other animals, the behaviour is still in many ways a mystery. While wardening the colony of Common Terns *S. hirundo* at Chesil Beach, Abbotsbury, Dorset, during 1948-50, I found two possible explanations for behaviour which might in the past have been attributed to 'dreads' or 'panics'. On the occasions concerned, I was always sufficiently near the colony to be able to detect the presence or absence of predators.

Brown hares *Lepus capensis* bred regularly on Chesil Beach. Although I never saw them disturb the nests or eggs of the terns, whenever one hopped leisurely through the colony the terns left the ground in alarm and panic. Since the hares were well camouflaged and partly hidden by prostrate plants, they would have been extremely difficult to detect from a distance.

The second explanation was of a more subtle nature. During hot, sultry weather, especially in the afternoon when the heat had built up on Chesil Beach, sometimes and quite suddenly a curious, whining noise could be heard coming in from the sea. This was always accompanied by a gust of wind, which came in over the beach, passed inland and disappeared as quickly as it had arrived. It lasted no longer than 15 seconds. A veritable hullabaloo followed these 'freak' winds and all the terns left the area for a while, before returning in small groups.

In October 1974 and May 1975 I visited the Meteorological Department of the Royal Naval Air Station, Portland, Dorset, in order to obtain information on these winds. I wish to express my sincere thanks to the Senior Meteorological Officer and his forecasting team for their help in drafting the following explanation. It is well known that if a thermal is released from the earth's surface it must be compensated by an inflow of air from all sides, which causes a temporary increase of surface wind towards the point of release of the thermal. Chesil Beach is possibly an ideal feature for the build-up of heat required for the formation of thermals, and each time that one is formed the surface wind will increase considerably for a very short period.   BERNARD KING
Gull Cry, 9 Park Road, Newlyn, Penzance, Cornwall

'Dreads' I have read Bernard King's note about 'dreads' at terneries (*Brit. Birds* 70: 81-82). His explanations of their cause, however, are too particularised to account for 'dreads' in general, and I submit the following as a broader possibility.

In any human crowd—for example at a football match—a moment of sudden silence occurs from time to time; the general hubbub stops and then, almost immediately, re-starts. At such times, I have often thought, 'Here, among birds, is where a "dread" would occur: they would frighten themselves by their own silence, and rise to see that all was well.'
                                                                      K. G. SPENCER
3 Landseer Close, off Carr Road, Burnley, Lancashire

Only a step from this are these fascinating accounts, which demonstrate that the enthusiastic spirit of bird watching persisted even through the appalling slaughter, tragedy and tedium of World War I, and that many birds did their best to carry on with their daily lives.

BIRDS AND SHELL-FIRE.

To the Editors of BRITISH BIRDS.

SIRS,—I have lately been reading various articles in the papers regarding birds in the war-stricken parts of France, so I thought you might care to have a few of my personal observations on this subject.

I will first enumerate the birds I have actually seen. These include the House-Sparrow, Swallow, House-Martin, Chaffinch, Yellow-Hammer, Sky-Lark, Willow-Wren, Magpie, Kestrel and Wood-Pigeon. All of these I have seen flying about in front of our own and the French artillery during an artillery duel. The House-Sparrows continue to sit on the house-tops of this village (I cannot name it), which is about ¾-mile from the French trenches, although the shells are continually knocking large holes in the roofs. So far I have only seen one of these birds killed at all.

Under the eaves of two of the cottages three pairs of House-Martins have already built their nests. (I may add that this village has had about twenty shells fired over and on it each day for the last two days. In fact it is only left standing because there are so many spies in it. We have caught three of them.)

A Magpie always seems to fly over our guns at about 9 a.m. each morning, while a Kestrel has appeared once.

Sky-Larks are continually up in the air, and are continually being mistaken at first sight for aeroplanes.

I heard a Willow-Wren at a point on a road about one mile east of Poperinghe. Swallows were also just on the outskirts of the same town. Chaffinches are quite numerous, and sing lustily when there is no cannonading. However, when lyddite shells are flying about, all the birds seem to realise that the ground is the only safe place for them, and accordingly they seek cover in the lowest parts of the hedges.

It is difficult to tell Wood-Pigeons sometimes from tame pigeons when they are at all high up. I think I have only seen one Wood-Pigeon, the rest are mostly pets kept by German gentlemen, one of whom, I may mention, was found in an attic here with six of his pets, and a note-book, and he swore he was English. PATRICK A. CHUBB.

2ND K.O.Y.L.I., B.E.F., FRANCE.
April 30*th*, 1915.

SIRS,—May I add a few notes (based on a brief sojourn in Flanders in 1915) to Mr. Chubb's observations in your June issue ? Articles in the Press have suggested that the fighting in France and Flanders would cause a widespread disturbance of bird-life. Personally, I doubt this very much, except along a zone at most three miles in width on each side of the firing-line.

Behind Ypres, things seemed quite normal, Larks, Tree-Pipits, Yellow Buntings and Common Whitethroats being the commonest birds observed in the fields. I spent two days in Ypres in July, at a time when it was being heavily shelled, and, except when a gun was fired very near them, the Sparrows, Greenfinches and Turtle-Doves in the trees on the ramparts seemed quite undisturbed ; many Swifts were nesting in the ruined towers, and I counted sixteen used House-Martins' nests on one side of the Cloth Hall. I noticed the same thing elsewhere in the case of Swallows and Sparrows nesting in a smashed farmhouse half-a-mile behind the fire-trenches. Other birds I saw near Ypres ramparts included Pied Wagtails, Spotted Flycatchers, Common Sandpipers, and by the moat an *Acrocephalus* with an unfamiliar song which I could not identify. I saw another *Acrocephalus* singing in some turnips gone to seed near Hooge, but only got a glimpse of it. The wet meadows in the salient always seemed full of Corncrakes at night, and in one wood close to Hooge there was always a chorus of birds at dawn (Chiffchaffs, Willow-Wrens, Wrens, Thrushes, etc.) in spite of the rifle fire on three sides, and I have heard Willow and Sedge-Warblers singing during an artillery duel.

Between the opposing lines birds were naturally scarce except Swallows, Swifts, stray Linnets, Pied and Yellow Wagtails, and Starlings (the great joy of our snipers when business is slack). I saw one pair of Tree-Sparrows nesting in a shell-torn tree between the lines, and once a Kingfisher appeared from nowhere and settled by a " Johnson hole " within five yards of our trench. In August at night I heard Curlew, Whimbrel, Green Sandpipers and Dunlins passing over the firing-line, and some Owl which I took to be a Little Owl.

ROYAL FREE HOSPITAL,   J. K. STANFORD.
    Sept. 5th, 1915.

But, like this Song-thrush, some found it just *too* unbearable at times!

SIRS,—In April, 1915, we discovered a Song-Thrush's nest built on a branch of a tree which had been cut and placed against the front of the steel shield of an 18 pr. gun in order to conceal it from view. The branch was actually touching the shield. The nest was built and three eggs were laid in spite of the fact that the gun was fired occasionally. But then there came a day when the gun was fired very frequently and this proved too much for the birds' nerves. They moved to a presumably quieter neighbourhood.

FLANDERS,   E. F. DELAFORCE,
    September 19th, 1915.   Lt. Col., R.F.A.

Even the serious business of the war at sea was momentarily put aside to allow for this observation of Red Grouse – surely the most land-lubberly of all British birds.

RED GROUSE FLYING OUT TO SEA.

ABOUT the last day of December, 1917, H.M. Destroyer *Ophelia* was on a course almost due east from Lerwick to Bergen. When at least thirty miles out at sea a covey of Red Grouse (*Lagopus scoticus*) flew to the ship and settled on deck. They were not seen till on the point of settling, so that their direction of flight was not ascertained. Lt. H. B. Anderson, R.N., who has lived on a grouse moor, and so of course knows the birds well, and Eng.-Commander A. K. Dibley were within ten yards of the covey, so that a mistake can hardly have been possible. Both these gentlemen have been communicated with and their accounts agree. The distance from Lerwick was calculated from the speed of the ship and the time from when land was left; the weather was calm and fine and the observers cannot remember any fog. A. H. R. WILSON.

[There are several instances given in the Scottish "Faunas" of Red Grouse crossing from island to island, the longest sea-passage being about eleven miles, from Scrabster to Hoy. They have also visited Bardsey Island twice, nearly twenty miles from their nearest habitat, though in this case the actual sea-passage need not have been more than two miles. In all of these land would have been in sight the whole journey from start to finish. Suitable ground appears to be very limited in extent in Shetland, and it may well have happened that it became overstocked during the war and so the birds were induced to seek fresh feeding grounds, as seems to have been the case in most of the instances above referred to. In such a species as the Red Grouse the wonderful faculty, by which migrating birds find their way, may be presumed to be at its lowest development, and whether or not these particular birds flew through a belt of fog after leaving land they seem to have hopelessly lost theirs.—N.F.T.]

Other game-birds (perhaps more used to the sound of twelve-bore cartridges) feature in this exchange of views on the function of the tail pattern.

Possible functions of the tail spots in the Woodcock Those who have handled Woodcock *Scolopax rusticola* for most of their lives often remain unaware that the glossy white spots on the tips of the tail feathers are white on only one side. On the dorsal surface these spots are brownish-grey, a hue which harmonises perfectly with the rest of the bird's beautifully camouflaged plumage. On the ventral side they are pure white and of a glistening appearance (plate 65a). Under a strong magnifying glass the glistening effect is shown to be due to the smooth, enamel-like texture of the under-surface of the shafts of the closely crowded, forward-pointing barbs. On their upper surfaces these barbs are not white but brownish-grey and are furnished along their entire length with very short, straight barbules of the same colour. It is these barbules which impart a soft velvety feeling to that part of the feather's surface.

The glossiness and intense whiteness of the tail spots have obviously been evolved to reflect even the faintest glimmer of light. But that,

of course, they can do only after the bird has rendered them visible by erecting its tail and spreading out its rectrices.

There must arise occasions in the life of such a beautifully camouflaged bird as the Woodcock (especially as it must derive further concealment from its nocturnal and crepuscular habits) when its virtual invisibility is neither necessary nor desirable: for example, during the male's courtship display on the ground. In *The Handbook* (4: 187) the findings of the few ornithologists who have observed this display are epitomised as follows: 'male struts round female with drooping wings, raised and spread tail and feathers of head and neck puffed out'. The effulgence of the strikingly conspicuous tail spots, when they are deliberately flaunted in front of the female, must greatly enhance the effectiveness of the bird's nuptial display.

As the white spots occur also in the plumage of the female, it is evident that they must also serve the species in some other way. Since a female Woodcock, when she attempts by injury-feigning to lure a potential predator away from her nest or nestlings, raises her tail and spreads out her rectrices, we may safely assume that the conspicuousness of the white tail spots, thus fully exposed to view, affords her valuable assistance by immediately attracting the predator's attention.

Besides the relatively large spots on the tips of the Woodcock's rectrices, some of the bird's undertail-coverts also have smaller, terminal white spots. These, unlike those on the rectrices, are white on both sides of the feather, a distinction which no doubt renders them visible from a greater number of angles. They apparently do not play an important part in any ritual display but, since Woodcock have been observed walking about with 'their tail cocked up like a crake's' (which would, of course, automatically

expose the undertail-coverts to view), we may safely conclude that one of their functions is to keep the birds visually in touch with one another. R. Wagstaffe (*in litt.*), of the Liverpool Museums, was reliably informed of a Woodcock which, whenever it was seen leading its chicks, as for instance across an open ride, always carried its tail in an erect position.   COLLINGWOOD INGRAM
The Grange, Benenden, Kent TN17 4DN

Function of the tail pattern in game-birds I was interested to read Collingwood Ingram's views (*Brit. Birds*, 67: 475-476) on the possible functions of the white tail spots in the Woodcock *Scolopax rusticola*.

White tips to the tail feathers are found in several species of gallinaceous birds, while many other species have lateral rectrices that are strikingly different in colour or pattern from the central tail feathers. The latter feature ensures that such patterns are visible only when the tail is spread. Duller central tail feathers are found also in several species of Charadriidae and Scolopacidae, for example the Killdeer *Charadrius vociferus*, which has white-tipped chestnut outer tail feathers and dull brown central feathers. The parallel between game-birds and certain waders appears to be carried further by the possession of pale tips on the undertail-coverts, seen in the Woodcock and in some 20 species in the families Tetraonidae and Phasianidae.

I have shown (*Ibis*, 118: 123-126) that, among game-birds, striking tail patterns are revealed when birds take flight, when a worried bird holds the tail in a spread position (behaviour which is particularly marked in the Bar-tailed Pheasant *Syrmaticus humiae*), and when females of certain species gather their broods. The undertail-coverts are revealed when a bird runs for cover and, to others in the rear, when an individual indulges in forward threat display. In all these circumstances, the patterns seem to represent intraspecific contact signals or following signals. Among dimorphic species, it is the females rather than the males that possess these plumage features, partly, no doubt, because they are often used between a female and her brood and partly because of the strong interrelationship between plumage and courtship behaviour in male game-birds.

Of the 36 gallinaceous species that show strong tail or undertail-covert patterns of the type described, about two-fifths live in forest areas and the rest in more open habitats. Four of the eight forest-dwelling species with brightly marked undertail-coverts are grouse, usually males, and, as in the Woodcock, the patterns seem mainly to be used in courtship. Nine of the ten open-country species with strong tail patterns belong to two genera, and they include the

Red-legged Partridge *Alectoris rufa* and the Partridge *Perdix perdix*. In these two species, the bright rufous outer rectrices may act as a visual signal between flying birds or to others remaining on the ground. For the rest, there seems to be a tendency for species of open habitats to have clear undertail-covert patterns, which would be visible at a distance, and for species of thickly vegetated habitats to have striking tail patterns, which would be visible when flying up from the forest floor. Females of three, or possibly four, pheasant species have both tail and undertail-covert patterns well developed, while, in a number of male grouse, the pale tips to the rectrices are used primarily in courtship.   G. W. H. DAVISON *School of Biological Sciences, University of Malaya, Kuala Lumpur, Malaysia*

The suggestion that birds spend time enjoying themselves is greeted with scorn by purists who believe that every action on the part of a wild creature must have a purpose. I cannot agree with this: man is 'allowed' to enjoy himself, so why not other creatures? I cannot prove that they *are* actively enjoying themselves, but then the opposite is equally difficult to demonstrate. Alternatively, if you argue that enjoyment is good for man – 'recharges the batteries' – why should it not serve the same function for other creatures? A good look at a sunbathing Blackbird, eyes half-closed, wings and tail outspread in abandoned luxury, or at Choughs or Ravens, tumbling about the sky in aerobatic ecstasy, should convince all but the most hardened that, however much it develops their flying skills, perhaps enjoyment does enter into birds' lives.

Kestrels 'playing' with airborne cardboard sheet   On a fine day in midsummer 1969, while seated near a high office window in the City of London, I watched two Kestrels *Falco tinnunculus* 'playing' with a drifting, airborne sheet of rigid cardboard roughly $1\frac{1}{2}$ m². The thermal airflow over the hot city had raised this heavy sheet to a height of about 100 m; it drifted slowly northwards while I watched for some three minutes, and it must have already been in the air for at least two minutes before I noticed it. It moved at a steady height, with slow oscillations, and the Kestrels' play was similarly languid, swooping slowly low above its upper surface or making more rapid, upcurving approaches almost to touch it with their beaks or wing-tips; they immediately soared high away when the sheet suddenly tumbled downwards and out of sight

below building level. Aerial play between certain crows (Corvidae), or between Kestrels and, for example, Jackdaws *Corvus monedula*, is well known; and the sometimes amazingly rapid pursuits to relatively high altitudes made by House Sparrows *Passer domesticus* after wind-blown feathers, easily recognisable as nest material, are also familiar. It seems surprising, however, that Kestrels should have so readily played with what must have been to them an alien object, perhaps 20 times their own size.

L. J. DAVENPORT
20 Ridgway, Mount Ararat Road, Richmond, Surrey TW10 6PR

SUN-BATHING HABIT OF JUVENILE GREAT-TITS.

DURING hot weather between July 11th and July 15th, 1945, I observed two juvenile Great Tits (*Parus major newtoni*) sun-bathing in my garden. It would appear that the hot sun and very dry earth encouraged these birds to develop a habit which was perhaps started when they were taking a dust-bath in the sun-baked soil.

While sun-bathing the birds lay motionless, breast to the ground, wings stretched out to the full, and tail feathers spread. On looking through field-glasses it could be seen that every feather on the back was puffed out. The breast seemed to be pressed tightly into the warm earth and the whole body appeared to be palpitating slowly. This sun-bathing position was assumed for about a minute at a time, after which the bird flew to a branch and commenced to preen its plumage.

The writer has always been under the impression that really hot sunshine caused distress to many birds, but it was quite obvious that these juvenile tits were enjoying the experience.

T. S. WILLIAMS.

[We do not think sun-bathing is really uncommon in Passerine birds, though little has been recorded about it and unless birds are tame or can be closely watched without their being aware of it, it is probably easily overlooked. In *Die Vögel Mitteleuropas*, Vol. i, O. and M. Heinroth, who reared a great many of the birds of central Europe in captivity, give photographs of a wide range of Passerine species thus occupied, namely Hawfinch, Snow-Finch, Wood-Lark, Pied Flycatcher, Black Redstart, White-spotted Bluethroat, Swallow and Sand-Martin. All the birds figured have the wings more or less spread and in some cases have assumed notably odd postures.—EDS.]

Anting, although often carried out with what appears to be the same enjoyment, is rather different.

"ANTING" OF STARLING.

ON October 24th, 1944, I watched at close range a Starling (*Sturnus v. vulgaris*) behaving strangely on the lawn. It was picking up something small from the grass and, with the object still in the tip of its bill, rubbing it vigorously on its thighs and the root of its tail under the tail feathers. At the same time the tail feathers were spread and agitated. Action was always swift and vigorous and was repeated several times. Binoculars showed that the object picked up was minute and light brown in colour. An examination of the exact spot on the lawn revealed that it swarmed with yellow ants, some carrying eggs. I have little doubt that the bird was deliberately preening itself with these.　　　　C. F. TEBBUTT.

[The singular behaviour which Mr. Tebbutt describes has attracted considerable attention in recent years, though this appears to be the first record of " anting " that has been sent to *British Birds*. The subject was discussed in detail by Mr. A. H. Chisholm (*Ibis*, 1944, pp. 389-405), who gives references to previous communications on the subject (though not, unfortunately, · a regular bibliography), the most important of these being *Ornithologische Monatsberichte*, 1935, pp. 134-8, and McAtee, *Auk*, 1938, pp. 98-105. The application of ants to the plumage has now been recorded for a considerable number of birds, and for the Starling more frequently than any : Mr. Chisholm mentions some twenty instances in Australia and it has been observed in America as well as in Europe. It must be admitted that the functional significance of the behaviour is still somewhat obscure, but of several possible explanations the most promising seems to be that the acid producd by the ants acts as a skin stimulant in a manner somewhat analogous to that of a dust-bath. It is also suggested that it may help to rid the skin of ectoparasites and that the pungent odour may itself be pleasurable to the birds, though the evidence for a well-developed sense of smell in most species is poor.—EDS.]

The fascination of this early note provoked a series of records of anting by different species.

"ANTING" BY MAGPIES.

In July, 1945, when staying in Co. Wicklow, I was much interested in the behaviour of a group of some 24 to 30 Magpies (*Pica p. pica*) from a neighbouring glen, which flew across the garden every evening and dropped on to a lawn where they occupied themselves in feeding, squabbling, etc. One or two generally came hopping up some steps which led from the lawn to a gravelled terrace and seemed to be busy on the steps. I examined the steps one evening before their visit and found the two top ones swarming with ants. That evening two birds came right up, so that I could distinctly see them from where I sat in a window. They collected the ants in their beaks and, raising their wings, tail and breast-feathers, etc., wiped the ants under the feathers until they were well covered. They then hopped back and joined the rest of the birds.   E. Reynolds.

"Anting" by Wryneck.—On July 1st, 1952, in my garden at Sutton Valence, Kent, I watched a Wryneck (*Jynx torquilla*) at a distance of about 8 yards. It was on a part of the lawn where there were many ants and where Wrynecks had been observed feeding on several occasions in 1951 and 1952. The bird was shuffling along the ground with half-open wings, shaking its wings and tail and apparently rubbing something into its plumage with its beak. It seems that this was an instance of "anting". The time was about 7 a.m., the weather fine and warm.   R. C. Stone.

"Anting" by Blackbird.—On August 3rd, 1953, at 1330 hours, I watched a ♀ Blackbird (*Turdus merula*) sitting on the gravel in front of my house at Edrom, Berwickshire, and picking up ants. It was seen to tuck them under both wings, next the body, and also at the root of the tail (on the top). It also sometimes ate the ants as well.   W. M. Logan Home.

"Anting" by Blackbird.—Shortly before 5 p.m. on September 4th, 1953, my wife and I saw a hen Blackbird (*Turdus merula*) on our lawn in Wimbledon going through the often reported actions of repeatedly picking up something from the ground and rubbing it under her wings and tail. The bird appeared in a state of ecstasy. We carefully marked the spot and on examination found the grass alive with small black ants in a great state of excitement.

W. P. C. TENISON.

"Anting" by House Sparrow.—At 2.40 p.m. on 16th August 1955 — a fine and warm afternoon — I watched a male House Sparrow (*Passer domesticus*) sitting on the pavement at Moor-lane, Plymouth, Devon. The bird was picking up ants, then rubbing them under its wings and tail with its beak.

A. M. COMMON

[We know of no previous published record of "anting" by a House Sparrow. The habit, however, has been noted in such closely-related species as certain of the weaver-birds (*Ploceidae*). —EDS.].

Before long, the possible reasons for such seemingly extraordinary behaviour were the subject of speculation. Among the suggestions put forward were the use of formic acid, produced by the ants, as a skin stimulant, perhaps enhancing vitamin production; or that the acid (or the ants themselves) served as a disinfectant, in the literal sense, ridding the bird of feather lice and other parasites. Such arguments were countered by behaviourists who felt that ants were picked up primarily as food and, discovering that they were obnoxious and awkward to handle, the bird tried to get rid of them, or at least render them harmless before eating them, resulting in the activities described as 'anting'. Derek Goodwin concisely summed up the response to this view, clearly indicating that 'anting' is primary, and any feeding secondary. Much remains to be discovered about this curious and fascinating behaviour.

"ANTING" BY BIRDS

SIRS,—The announcement by the Editors of *British Birds* (*antea*, vol. xlvii, pp. 312-313), based on the work of H. Poulsen, that "anting" by birds is "quite automatic" and is merely performed to rub off formic acid or any other irritant from the head is likely to be taken as an *ex-cathedra* pronouncement by many who have not closely observed this behaviour. May I therefore briefly state some reasons why I am very far from being in agreement with the above theory?

(1) Some birds that show intense anting behaviour do not eat worker ants, but discard them after use.

(2) The Jay (*Garrulus glandarius*) Green Magpie (*Cissa chinensis*) and Blue Magpie (*Urocissa erythrorhyncha*) do not pick up ants in bill when anting.

(3) The Rook and Carrion Crow (*Corvus frugilegus* and *C. corone*) have special movements which involve lying "spread-eagled" among the ants (see *Ibis,* vol. 97, pp. 147-149).

(4) The Jay's reaction to irritation on (?or near) the eye is to rub the eye on top of the shoulder. This is not an anting movement (it is shown in identical form by many birds, such as pigeons, which never ant) but the bird will use it whilst anting if formic acid gets on its eye.

(5) The Starling (*Sturnus vulgaris*) when anting picks up ant after ant until it has a large ball of them in the tip of its bill. This behaviour is quite different to that meted out to hairy or distasteful insects being prepared for food, which are swallowed or discarded before the next is picked up.

(6) Game-birds which—unlike most Passerines—often eat worker ants, *and which habitually dust-bathe,* do not ant, although they react in the same way as the Jay when formic acid gets on their eye.

That under certain circumstances irritants applied to a bird's face may serve as a releaser for the anting movements—especially in captive birds that have been long denied the opportunity of anting—I do not for a moment doubt. It may even be that anting had its origin in efforts to remove formic acid, although this is difficult to reconcile with the very different movements employed by species which do not ant (and some that do, when not in anting mood), just as nest-building seems to have originated in displacement movements and re-directed aggressiveness, but in its present form it is, in my opinion, a very distinct behaviour pattern, unconnected with feeding.   DEREK GOODWIN.

'Smoke-bathing' is the subject of similar discussion and uncertainty.

"SMOKE-BATHING" OF STARLING.

A NOTE on the "anting" of the Starling (*Sturnus v. vulgaris*) (*antea,* Vol. xxxix, p. 84) and mention of it in Vol. xl, p. 85, prompts me to add that I have on several occasions noted what I take to be analogous behaviour in these birds, that is, their habit of perching on the lee side of a chimney, allowing the smoke to blow over them, on occasions shuffling their feathers as though encouraging the smoke to penetrate all parts of their plumage.

I have also a note referring to this behaviour in the Rook (*Corvus f. frugilegus*), which the writer (Colin Macdonald) says he has seen take place. The probable connexion between the two habits of the rather verminous Starling seems to be worth noting.

                                          ROGER C. PRIDEAUX.

[It should be noted that, as Chisholm has shown (*Ibis,* 1944, pp. 389-405), there are considerable objections to the "anti-parasite" theory as a general explanation of "anting." The alternative suggestion that weak acids have a stimulating effect on the skin, which is agreeable to the birds, would presumably apply also to smoke.—EDS.]

Rarely are bird watchers short of convincing explanations for the activities of the birds under observation.

Trembling movements of House Martin when nest-building

On 6th June 1975, near South Gorley, Hampshire, I watched at close range with binoculars a House Martin *Delichon urbica* building its nest, which was in the early stages of construction. The nest was situated below the eaves of an old thatched cottage at a height of three metres from the ground. I noticed that, when the martin placed and held in position with its beak a mud-pellet, its head and body trembled violently for about three seonds. These movements ceased when the bill was carefully withdrawn. On 10th June, I visited the site again and noted the same movements each time mud-pellets were added to the nest.   HUBERT E. POUNDS
27 Orchard Close, Ringwood, Hampshire BH24 ILP

This behaviour, although not widely recorded, is quite normal. It is apparently similar to the quivering or trembling movements used by most species of birds when attempting to fix material in place, at least during some stage of nest building. EDS

As stated in the editorial comment (*Brit. Birds* 69: 451), it is quite normal for House Martins to make quivering or trembling movements when nest-building. This behaviour was noted by Gilbert White (*The Natural History of Selborne*, Letter XVI, 20th November 1773): 'These industrious artificers are at their labours in the long days before four in the morning: when they fix their materials they plaster them on with their chins, *moving their heads with a quick vibratory motion*' (my italics).

K. G. SPENCER
3 Landseer Close, off Carr Road, Burnley, Lancashire

But the answer is not usually as eminently practical as the one offered by Mr Spencer:

Trembling movements of House Martin when nest-building

A recent note by Hubert E. Pounds (*Brit. Birds* 69: 451) drew attention to the behaviour of nesting House Martins *Delichon urbica* as they place each pellet of mud in position: there is a rapid vibratory movement of the head. While I cannot prove it, I suspect that this action causes the water in the mud to flow, thereby ensuring better bonding. Building contractors, when laying big concrete foundations, frequently insert a vibrating rod into the mass of wet concrete in order to assist it to flow and settle. I suggest that the head actions of the House Martins would have a similar effect.

ROBERT SPENCER
British Trust for Ornithology, Beech Grove, Tring, Hertfordshire HP23 5NR

How many of us give much thought to *where* the multitudes of birds – of many shapes, sizes and habits – that surround us during the day, go at night? The spectacular myriads of Starlings wheeling against a winter evening before descending into city centres, or patches of woodland, to seek safety and shelter come to mind readily, but what of other birds? Where do *they* roost? In ones and twos, or in flocks? How far do they travel to reach their roost? For many birds, our knowledge remains surprisingly scanty, although, for some, the documentation is better – and fascinating!

A LARGE RAVEN ROOST.

WHILST on a visit to the Westmorland Pennines on June 28th, 1925, accompanied by Mr. E. Blezard, we traversed a dale which terminated in a long series of limestone crags. From these we disturbed three Ravens (*Corvus corax*), and an examination of the place disclosed a large amount of droppings and loose feathers scattered the whole length of the rocks, unmistakably the product of this species. This evidence, coupled with the secluded nature of the locality, suggested to us an habitual roosting haunt of these birds, and determined us to again visit these crags on some future occasion.

This we were able to do on September 28th, 1925. When we reached the vicinity of the crags in the late afternoon, approaching them from an adjoining fell top, we disturbed in the first instance three Ravens, but on gaining higher ground we observed several others flying about the limestone scar and dale sides, and soon had ten under observation. Still proceeding towards the crags we noticed other Ravens to be leaving the dale head and joining this first party, until we were able to count seventeen birds.

Ravens continued to pass down the dale, singly or in pairs, until our number had reached twenty-three, and finally a party of four joined these, making a total of twenty-seven Ravens.

The flight of these twenty-seven birds when gathered together can only be described as winged confusion, birds flying in every direction, some lifting high in the air above their fellows, others almost hugging the crags and valley sides, whilst several flew low over the fell in our direction, but all seemed reluctant to leave the dale head, only gradually drifting down towards the foot of the valley as we approached at the opposite end.

Most, if not all, of the birds were calling during the forty-five minutes or so which we had them under observation.

R. GRAHAM.

LARGE RAVEN ROOST IN PERTHSHIRE.

EACH winter since the war a crag only a mile and a quarter from the village of Pitlochrie, Perthshire, and another rock within 300 yards of it have been occupied by very large numbers of Ravens (*Corvus c. corax*). The birds go out to the east every morning and return to roost at nights from the east and north-east. The biggest number counted on one night was a hundred and twenty two winters ago. On April 18th, 1943, eighty were counted and on May 1st forty, all in pairs on both dates. By May 3rd they had left. They also left very late in the season in 1941 and 1942. Mr. Seton Gordon suggests that the birds are migrants from Scandinavia.

E. J. FERGUSSON.

LARGE GATHERING OF RAVENS DURING BREEDING SEASON.

On March 27th, 1946, I saw an unusually large gathering of Ravens (*Corvus c. corax*) near Cwmanne, in Carmarthenshire. About 40-50 birds were present on a hillside which contained several fir-plantations and a small, disused slate-quarry ; most of the birds appeared to be paired and there was continual croaking and display, with birds present in the air, on the ground and perching in the conifers. Sheep were grazing the hillside but no carcases were seen and the birds were present on several other occasions during the same week.

The Raven is a fairly common resident in the district, but such a large gathering during the normal breeding-season would seem to be unusual. No birds were found to be breeding in the immediate neighbourhood.

DEREK K. BRYSON.

[On April 14th, 1933, I counted thirty-one Ravens together in the air in the Cumberland mountains and there were probably others on the ground. Although these were seen in the breeding-season at a date later than those in Wales there is no doubt that they had been attracted by dead sheep which had been buried by a heavy snowfall and were only then uncovered.—A.W.B.]

A CUMBERLAND MAGPIE ROOST.

During one winter, at least, a Cumberland roost of the Magpie (*Pica p. pica*) was similar in size to the North Yorkshire roost described by Capt. J. P. Utley (*antea* p. 159.)

The place used is a very steep bank, a mile long and sixty feet high, where the River Eden cuts against a glacial ridge on which stands the village of Beaumont, four miles north-west of Carlisle. It is thickly clothed with tall deciduous trees, mainly ash, sycamore, beech and alder with a few pines. Thorns grow sparsely beneath them, and at the northern end where the bank merges into a narrow strip of salt marsh leading to one of the extensive Solway marshes, there is a thicket of old, dense thorns.

The Magpies favoured the northern half, the one farthest from the village, and rough counts gave well over 200 of them seen to come in on December 27th, 1926, and again on January 1st, 1927. On both dates the flight began while it was still quite light and ended at dark. It was all from the other side of the river, that is from the east, no birds being seen to enter by the top of the bank from the west. From as far as they could be seen over the flat fields, single birds to small parties came in a straggling procession across the water to crowd into both tall trees and thorn bushes. They crossed and entered well below the topmost tree line. It is not known how far and wide they came from beyond the flat land where, in daytime, no more than say up to half-a-dozen Magpies were to be seen. Even the whole countryside to the eastern limits of the county is sparsely populated by comparison with the land to the west, where the Magpie is really common. By December 2nd, 1928, the roost had fallen off somewhat, but it was still a strong one.

In November 1931 the roost was again occupied by some numbers of Magpies. In one shot at 4.0 a.m. the stomach had by that time become completely empty.

Before daylight on February 2nd, 1935 a lot of Magpies were heard chattering in the roost, and this is the last date on which numbers were noted.

Up till darkness on the afternoon of January 3rd, 1943 no Magpies came in to roost. Two or three were chattering at 5.15 as they settled in a hedge beyond the river.

In an appendix to " Lakeland Ornithology 1892-1913 " by E. B. Dunlop (*Trans. Carlisle Nat. Hist. Soc.*, Vol. 3, 1923) L. E. Hope says that in the winter of 1912 he and Dunlop visited a roosting place of Magpies near Kirkbride where at least one hundred birds habitually gathered in a tall hedgerow. Kirkbride is situated in the previously mentioned quarter where Magpies are numerous.

ERNEST BLEZARD.

The Pied Wagtail roost in a tree in the centre of Dublin is justly famous, and publication of photographs of it provoked a double response:

PIED WAGTAIL ROOST ON A LEICESTER BUILDING.

IT is now known that a large number of Pied Wagtails (*Motacilla a. yarrellii*) have for the past two years used the glass roof of the branch Post Office in Campbell Street, Leicester, as their winter roosting quarters. The Post Office in question is less than a hundred yards from the London Midland and Scottish Railway station and the main street, and six hundred yards from the centre of the City of Leicester.

The glass roof on which the birds roost consists of three gables, and the whole roof is overlooked on all four sides by the windows of a corridor at the same level. I first saw the birds at roost in February, 1935, when they were at full strength, numbering from four to six hundred. It was an amazing spectacle. The tops of the roof gables and surrounding window ledges were lined with Wagtails, and dense masses of them squatting flat on the sloping panes of glass, quite undisturbed by frequent and sudden illumination from, or persons appearing at, the aforementioned windows.

During March and April, by the courtesy of the Post Office officials, I have been able to keep the roof under constant observation and on some occasions while the birds were coming in to roost. They arrived in small groups, generally three or four, in most cases dropping into the vicinity of the roof from a considerable height, thus giving little or no indication of the direction from which they had come. On one occasion only, from a point about three hundred yards distant, did I observe a flight of Wagtails (five in all) making in the direction of the roost.

On April 18th I received reliable information from an interested Post Office official that the birds were still in occupation, but in slightly reduced numbers.

On May 1st I visited the roost myself at 9.15, shortly after dusk, expecting to find the roost deserted, but was surprised that I was able to count upwards of two hundred roosting Wagtails. The roost was still occupied on May 8th, but on May 25th it was deserted.

W. E. MAYES,
Leicester Museum.

PIED WAGTAIL ROOST IN GORSE.

INFORMATION as to the sites of winter roosts of the Pied Wagtail (*Motacilla a. yarrellii*) is curiously scanty, and it might well be suggested here that other observers come forward with information as to sites other than reed-beds, which are well known as favourite roosting-places of Pied and Yellow (*Motacilla f. rayi*) Wagtails. The Pied Wagtail tree-roost in the centre of Dublin has been described in *British Birds*, Vol. XXIV., pp. 26-8, and Vol. XXVI., p. 93, and in *Irish Nat. Jour.* V., pp. 162-3, while one in a rhododendron, recorded in the *Journal of the Derbyshire Arch. & Nat. Hist. Soc.*, 1933, was referred to in *B.B.*, XXVIII., p. 32.

On January 12th, 1935, I found a roost of between 600 and 1,000 Pied Wagtails in a thick growth of gorse (*Ulex europœus*) in a rushy field near Martletwy, Pembrokeshire. The gorse was between 4 feet and 6 feet high and situated close to a hedge bordering a second-class country road. The nearest buildings were 120 yards away and the district is rather remote and unfrequented.

The birds assembled soon after sunset and their great numbers on the road near the roost first attracted my attention. They roosted well down among the prickly shoots, so that a flashlight photograph would have been almost impossible. The roost was still occupied in force up to March 8th, when I had to discontinue my observations.

R. M. LOCKLEY.

Many years later, the versatility of Pied Wagtails was better known, and several roosts – notably one at Reading sewage farm – were well studied.

Another typical site was found to be greenhouses, where the sensible birds congregated from miles around for warmth and safety.

Unusual roosting site of Pied Wagtails.—On 3rd September 1959 a large roost of Pied Wagtails (*Motacilla alba*) was found inside greenhouses used for growing tomatoes at Milton near Cambridge. The birds entered through the open windows in the roof and roosted on the guiding wires and on the tomato plants themselves at a height of eight to fourteen feet. The owners of the greenhouses said that the birds were usually present in large numbers from July until early November, and again in smaller numbers in the spring. The practice apparently first began about five years ago and much damage is caused by the birds' fouling the plants, particularly in the spring when these are small, and also the fruit.

During the seven weeks following our first visit to the roost, six excursions were made there at night and 453 Pied Wagtails were ringed. Of these, 244 were adult and 209 first-winter, but of the last 83, caught on 22nd and 24th October, 39 were adult (21 males and 18 females) and 44 were first-winter (25 males and 19 females). There were also 21 retraps of birds ringed at another Cambridge roost in the previous two winters. It was estimated that between 600 and 800 wagtails were present during September 1959, and after that numbers gradually declined to 50 at the end of October, when the roost finally dispersed because of the removal of the plants and the closing of the windows. These peak figures are supported by the numbers of retraps: for example, on 27th September, when 268 birds had already been ringed, only 25% of a catch of 186 had rings on.

It is interesting to note that when the wagtails abandon the greenhouse roost they disperse to several smaller roosts in more typical reed-bed sites and it was at one of these that the birds from the previous two winters had been ringed. Similarly, a large proportion of those caught in November 1959 at this roost, which is 4 miles S.E. of the greenhouses, had been ringed in the greenhouses in September and October. Some indication of the size of the area from which the large September roost draws its members may be given by the fact that one wagtail was recovered seven miles away the day after it was ringed. In addition, towards the end of 1959, wagtails with rings on were reported following the plough on farms as far as nine miles away from Milton. Evidence that even passage birds join the roost inside the greenhouses is provided by one ringed on 7th September 1959 and recovered on 26th October in southern Spain.

Finally, seven of the birds ringed at the reed-bed roost in the winter of 1957-58 were found dead together in the Milton greenhouses during cold weather on 16th February 1958, at the same time as many un-ringed ones. They had apparently entered for warmth during severe weather and had either been unable to get out or been too weak to do so. This use of the greenhouses at that time of the year is apparently quite exceptional.   C. D. T. MINTON

This 'safety', however, proved to be a mixed blessing at one Hampshire site. The greenhouse ventilation was automatically controlled, and on chilly evenings the vents would close before latecomers arrived. These stragglers were forced to shelter under the ridges and eaves of the greenhouse, where the local Barn Owl soon learned to hunt them out.

The Long-tailed Tit is a very small bird which, despite its fluffy insulating feathers, is at risk on cold nights, and a common victim of severe winters. The laws of physics tell us that small birds are liable to disproportionately high heat loss, and that a larger, spherical body is far better for energy conservation. This, as far as the roost site allows, the tits try to achieve:

ROOSTING BEHAVIOUR OF LONG-TAILED TITS.

I CAN confirm D. B. Grubb's account (*antea*, Vol. xxxviii, p. 54) of the roosting of Long-tailed Tits (*Ægithalos caudatus rosaceus*). On December 24th, 1944, in dull but by no means cold weather, I found a party of five just before dusk in the hedge of one of the Severn meadows at Powick, near Worcester. In the next 10 minutes they worked their way to the rough hedges of a neighbouring green lane. They were now quite silent, very close together, and not nearly so active as before. Then all of them flew for a few yards down the lane and entered a bramble-patch (16.25, G.M.T.). I was now able to watch them at about six feet. Two of them were perched side by side on a stem about four feet six inches from the ground in the middle of the bramble-patch, which was about six feet high. The two birds shuffled backwards and forwards, now facing one way, now the other, but always keeping close together. When they had finally settled down a third bird dropped down between them and the shuffling was repeated. Finally, the other two joined them and more similar shuffling followed, accompanied now by a few quiet "tupp" notes. The birds were now perched close together in a row along the bramble stem. Everything was quiet for a few moments ; then a Blackbird arrived on the other side of the bramble-bush and started "spink-ing." One of the Long-tailed Tits flew towards the Blackbird, using the churring "tsirrrp" note and drove it off. The other tits had separated, but soon settled down again on a branch about six inches above the original position. The valiant one waited in the old position while the rest shuffled about for a short time and then joined the party. There was a little more movement before all was quiet (16.40, G.M.T.). It was now almost dark ; as far as I was able to see, however, the birds were now roosting with heads together and tails outside. JOHN TOOBY.

Treecreepers are similarly vulnerable, but resolve their problems alone, often in a fascinating way. The holes they make are oval, and roughly the size of a hard-boiled hen's egg cut lengthwise. It seems that there are now few Wellingtonias (which have a soft, springy bark almost like peat fibre) without Treecreeper roosting holes: all the more remarkable in the light of the Rev. Savage's comment that this tree was not introduced to Britain until 1853.

ROOSTING HABIT OF THE TREE-CREEPER.

IN September, 1922, Mr. K. C. Pryor drew my attention to a number of small holes in the trunks of the Wellingtonias in a garden near Bassenthwaite, mid-Cumberland, which, from the droppings below each hole, were obviously tenanted by some bird. He says that he went at dusk and found each one occupied by a Tree-Creeper (*Certhia familiaris brittanica*).

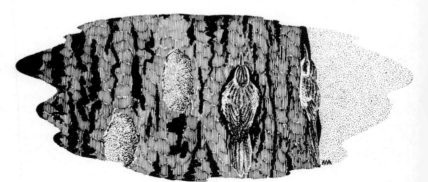

It clung in such a position that its back was on a level with the rugged bark of the tree, its beak pointing straight upward.

The holes are evidently made by the birds themselves in the soft bark ; and, in the trees I examined both there and also here in north Cumberland, were between four and eight feet from the ground.

There are several on each tree and only those on the lee side are occupied.

Mr. Pryor tells me that his mother has since found similar holes in the Wellingtonias in Co. Kilkenny, S.W. Ireland ; and in the *Irish Naturalist,* January, 1923 [Vol. XXXII., No. 1, page 1], there is a description, with photograph, of these roosting holes by Mr. Nevin H. Foster, observed in Co. Down, N.E. Ireland.   From this it would appear that the habit is a general and not a local one.

The tree in question, the Wellingtonia (*Sequoia gigantea*), was not, according to Johnson's *Gardeners' Dictionary,* introduced into this country until 1853.   So that the habit is evidently a recent one.   E. U. Savage.

❧ 2 ❧
Food and Feeding

It is tempting to assume that, by now, we must know just about everything there is to know about the diet of most of our birds. Watching birds feeding would seem to be one of the simplest of studies for the bird watcher, but is it always so? The answer may be 'yes' in the case of Fieldfares, for example, handsome in winter feeding on hawthorn berries or rotting fruit on the orchard floor, but what is it that the Curlew probes deep into the estuarine mud to reach? All we see is the throat movement as some tasty morsel – shellfish? worm? – slides down. Birds are opportunists, too, and as we (and they) live in a changing environment we should expect to be able to record new food-stuffs or feeding techniques. Relatively few birds have a diet that is both specialised and restricted in scope – on the contrary, most are catholic in their tastes, always ready to sample and exploit fresh opportunities. Beyond this, although we can often make generalised statements about diet, detailed information (how often? how much? how important?) is, surprisingly, still lacking.

The Golden Eagle, for example, is a well-known and well-studied bird, but its feeding territory is so enormous and accurate observation in mountain terrain so difficult that much of the information on its diet is apocryphal. This is especially true of that fascinating (but dangerous) area surrounding its ability to tackle large prey, and whether or not it is a regular lamb killer.

Golden Eagle persistently attacking red deer calf On 26th June 1976, I watched a pair of Golden Eagles *Aquila chrysaetos* hunting over a mountain ridge above Loch Hourn, Highland, where several female red deer *Cervus elaphus* and their calves were grazing. The eagles flew out of sight to the east, but several minutes later the female returned and descended vertically and rather slowly, with her wings half-closed and her legs fully extended below. She landed in a slight depression, where she may have been attempting to kill a deer calf which was lying there, but three hinds rushed up, causing her to take off. Later, I saw the male eagle hanging motionless on outstretched wings above the ridge; below him, his mate was diving repeatedly, at an angle of 45 degrees, at the same deer calf, which was running about frantically as the eagle dived at its back from one side and then pulled up, turned and dived again from the other; once the eagle briefly held on to the calf's back. The hind was running up and down close to her young, trying to distract the eagle, which broke off the attack after several passes and settled briefly on a rock before she and her mate flew off east again. I had not seen the eagle's approach for the attacks, but assumed that she flew east after spotting the calf and then doubled back on the far side of the mountain, so as to gain an element of surprise by coming up over the ridge directly above her intended prey.

C. J. NORTHEAST
23 Ffordd Colomendy, Denbigh, Clwyd

Seton Gordon (1955, *The Golden Eagle: King of Birds*) described a number of attacks by Golden Eagles on red deer calves, but these were all second-hand stories related to him by deer-stalkers. EDS

Golden Eagle killing red deer calf I am prompted by C. J. Northeast's note (*Brit. Birds* 71: 36-37) to draw attention to A. Baxter Cooper's excellent first-hand account of an immature Golden Eagle *Aquila chrysaetos* killing and attempting to lift a young red deer *Cervus elaphus* weighing 20.5 kg (*J. Zool. Lond.* 158: 215-216).

IAN D. PENNIE
5 Badcall, Scourie, Sutherland IV27 4TH

Have they the physique – the sheer lifting power – to exploit such large prey even if they can kill it?

LIFTING AND WEIGHT-CARRYING POWER OF GOLDEN EAGLES.

To the Editors of BRITISH BIRDS.

SIRS,—From time to time discussions arise on this question. It would be interesting to learn if any of your readers have had personal experience, or obtained authentic records of actual weights lifted and carried by Golden Eagles. In a recent letter to *The Times* the writer, Mr. L. Ropner, of Stockton, states that whilst fishing on Loch Shiel, he saw an Eagle swoop, take up a fawn, and glide down the mountain side for about half a mile.

G. WITHERINGTON.

19. SUMNER PLACE, S.W.7.

LIFTING POWER OF THE GOLDEN EAGLE.

To the Editors of BRITISH BIRDS.

SIRS.—When I was filming the Golden Eagle two and three years ago I had good opportunities of observing the weight-lifting powers of the bird. In one eyrie there was a lamb not less than a fortnight old, and at another I saw the male Eagle bring mountain hares to the nest. On one of his visits he was flying at a height of about 500 feet and seemed to be carrying the hare with the greatest ease ; and on another occasion he flew across the great valley beneath the nest, and it looked as if the hare made no difference to his flight or speed of travelling. Also he had no difficulty in landing at the nest with these burdens.

In my opinion, an Eagle with its full flight-feathers, that is, providing it is not moulting, would have no difficulty in carrying hares or young lambs distances of two or three miles. OLIVER G. PIKE.
LEIGHTON BUZZARD.

To the Editors of BRITISH BIRDS.

SIRS,—I am convinced this question needs a great deal more investigation. I have lived in Golden Eagle country all my life almost and I think it is a very remarkable thing how seldom one sees the Eagle strike down or carry its prey. During the summer of 1924 I watched for three days at an eyrie in sheep country. There were three or four lambs in the eyrie, all in an advanced stage of decomposition, and the shepherd was quite certain that all these lambs were stillborn ones. During the summer of 1925 my wife and I watched at an Eagle's eyrie almost daily for twelve weeks of the Eaglets' nestling period. During this time the heaviest prey brought was roe-deer calves, four of which met their end. They may, of course, have been left by their does or even stillborn ; even to see a certain animal in the eyrie does not prove that the Eagle actually *killed* it. The ease with which Eagles can be caught in traps baited with hares or cats shows that they like carrion. The blue hares brought to this eyrie were generally brought from above. The eyrie was situated about 1,500 ft. above the sea, with hills 2,000 ft. higher up and forest 500 ft. below. The roe-deer calves must all have been found not less than 500 ft. *below* the nest.

On June 28th my wife was in the hide when a roe calf was brought. I should mention that the eyrie was in a tree on a very steep hillside. Judging by the behaviour of the young Eaglets at 10.45 on this day the cock Eagle landed on a tree *below* the tree on which the eyrie was situated. Here, to the indignation of the Eaglets, the cock remained for a quarter of an hour. Then with much flapping, heard by my wife, the cock flew up the steep hillside and landed on the edge of the eyrie, carrying the roe calf in one foot. He was quite exhausted and had his beak wide open for several minutes, although he had rested for a quarter of an hour in a neighbouring tree. The calf was under a week old but was minus the head and part of the entrails. At this eyrie we noticed that the prey was always carried in one foot. It appears that the evidence on this subject is conflicting, and probably a great deal depends on the actual circumstances, such as wind and position of the prey ; but the day my wife observed the roe calf being brought there was no wind to help the Eagle and this may account for his exhaustion.

This season I hope to make some more observations from a hide and if possible to weigh some of the prey brought to the eyrie.

SETON GORDON.

WEIGHT-CARRYING POWER OF THE GOLDEN EAGLE.

SIRS,—With reference to the letter on this subject (*antea*, p. 24), an experience of mine in the Himalayas may be of interest. In May and June 1893 I was shooting ibex in the Wakha nullah in Ladak, beyond Cashmere, and one evening while returning to camp, I disturbed a Golden Eagle feeding round a bend in a stream-bed. The Eagle rose and flew off, carrying something heavy in his claws. He flew low, about 50 feet up but fairly easily, and pitched about half a mile further up the stream. On following him up with my shot-gun, he rose from round another bend, again carrying his burden about, 30 yards from me, and I dropped him easily. He proved to be a fine Golden Eagle and his prey a very large marmot. I took both to my camp and weighed them at once, as I was so struck with the size of the marmot and was amazed that the Eagle had carried him, comparatively speaking, so easily. Unfortunately I cannot at the moment gain access to the notes and sketches I made at the time, but two things I can be absolutely certain of are, that the marmot was heavier than the Eagle and that their respective weights were round about 11 and 10 lbs., the Eagle being just under or just over 10 lbs. and the marmot about 1 lb. more. Of course the weight of the marmot was much less than that of the lamb carried by the Eagle described in your former correspondent's letter, but on the other hand my Eagle was far from being laden to the full extent of his carrying powers. H. DELMÉ-RADCLIFFE.

This fascinating account of what could be called 'play' gives an indication of the value to predators of practising their skills.

Golden Eagle repeatedly catching sticks in flight On 12th January 1975, on the Isle of Mull, Strathclyde, I noticed an immature Golden Eagle *Aquila chrysaetos* flying over an oak-wood. It was carrying a stick about 1 m long and was pecking at it so furiously that at first I thought

that the stick was entangled in its talons. At a range of about ⅓ km, I could see twigs and pieces of bark being carried away in the wind. The eagle maintained its position by hovering, but on one occasion it became so obsessed with the stick that it appeared to stall and roll like a Raven *Corvus corax* before regaining balance. After a few minutes it landed with the stick on a bare hillside, just out of sight, but soon reappeared, with the stick still in its talons. Shortly thereafter, it descended to the hill again, but this time, when it rose, it was carrying the stick in its bill. Rising on the wind, it transferred the stick to its talons, took up a position about 50 m above the hill, and started a 'game' which lasted for at least ten minutes. The eagle dropped the stick and plummeted down, catching it before reaching the ground, then rose again to a similar height, dropped the stick, but failed to catch it before it landed. The eagle flew up with a fresh stick and proceeded to trim the twigs as before. The new stick was dropped and retrieved successfully six times in succession; the seventh attempt failed and the stick landed on the hillside. The eagle landed and tossed it about with sharp movements of its bill. It then took off and repeated the procedure as before. I watched ten successive successful stoops before I left. RICHARD COOMBER

Even the majestic – and supposedly noble – Golden Eagle must lower its sights occasionally, and turn to more mundane, even seemingly obnoxious, food:

Golden Eagle eating Fulmars On the Isle of Eigg, Lochaber, Highland, a pair of Golden Eagles *Aquila chrysaetos* apparently nests on the 100-metre north-west-facing sea cliffs, a haunt more typical of the White-tailed Eagle *Haliaetus albicilla*. During a fortnight's stay on the island in late August 1972, I discovered food remains on a ledge on these cliffs that was used as a feeding base by one of the eagles. The three pellets present contained a skull of a Rabbit *Oryctolagus cuniculus*, a complete beak and some feathers of a Fulmar *Fulmarus glacialis*, and assorted bones of both species. Beside these lay a complete and freshly stripped skeleton of a second Fulmar still bearing drops and smears of unclotted blood.

Dr D. A. Bannerman (1956, *The Birds of the British Isles*, vol. 5) mentioned both Bald Eagles *H. leucocephalus* and Peregrines *Falco peregrinus* taking Fulmars; while the late James Fisher (1952, *The Fulmar*) recorded Bald and White-tailed Eagles as major predators of this species. In view of the presence of large numbers of Rabbits over the whole of the island, it would appear rather curious that the Golden Eagles on Eigg should take Fulmars, firstly because of their relative scarcity and secondly because of the difficulty of catching them while avoiding the oil ejected by the victims (see, e.g., *Brit. Birds*, 67: 297-301). The possibility of a Peregrine having made the kills cannot be ruled out, though no Peregrines were seen on Eigg by myself and my two companions during our stay. DAVID M. HAWKER

David Lea has seen dead Fulmars at or close by the Golden Eagle eyrie on Hoy, Orkney (see page 262), and the late E. Balfour told him of an incident he had witnessed of an eagle on Hoy actually taking a Fulmar in flight; it is also known in the Inner Hebrides. Leslie H. Brown, in a paper on Golden Eagles in north-west Sutherland (*Brit. Birds*, 62: 345-363), stated (page 355) that 'one pair of eagles fed extensively on Fulmars *Fulmarus glacialis* in late June and July [1967], and must have travelled eight to ten miles to catch them; the nest could be located by the smell of Fulmars'; but no evidence of Fulmar prey could be found in the eyries of the 17 other pairs studied, and incidentally there was no evidence at all of gulls being eaten. Eds

Fulmars are notoriously aggressive birds (p 171) so here one can imagine either extreme hunger as the driving force, or perhaps an acquired aptitude for coping in such difficult circumstances.

Most birds of prey probably depend far more than we would like to imagine on very small prey – worms, beetles and the like – and most will not reject easily available carrion. In going for less likely foods, obviously their intrinsic opportunism will show – sometimes to startling effect.

Kestrel apparently attempting to catch Goldfish In 1974 a Kestrel *Falco tinnunculus* nested in a beech coppice near my house near Blackboys, East Sussex, and frequently hunted for beetles and mice in the ha-ha which divides my garden from a field of barley. Near the ha-ha and 14 metres from my window is an ornamental pond inhabited by Goldfish *Carassius auratus*. The Kestrel used a tree by the pond as a lookout post. On 8th October 1974 I saw it swoop vertically from the tree to the pond in an apparent attempt to catch one of the numerous fish which I had seen a few moments before, basking in the shallows. It failed, though both feet touched the water. I do not believe that Goldfish have previously been recorded as potential prey for this species. The pond had no frogs or voles, and it was too late in the season for it to have been likely that an aquatic insect had attracted the Kestrel.   GUY MOUNTFORT
Plovers Meadow, Possingworth Park, Blackboys, Uckfield, East Sussex

FOOD OF KESTREL AND POSSIBLE SEED-DISPERSAL.

ON June 17th, 1936, I was shown a nest of a Kestrel (*Falco t. tinnunculus*) containing two young, in an elm near Farnham Royal (Bucks). A number of bones, obviously the remains of the Kestrel's prey were found. These bones were identified for me at the Natural History Museum, South Kensington, and they represent approximately the following numbers of individuals :

Twenty-two common field-voles (*Microtus agrestis hirtus*) ; one water-vole (*Arvicola amphibius*) ; one field-mouse (*Apodemus sylvaticus*) ; four young rats (*Rattus* sp?) ; four House Sparrows (*Passer domesticus*).

A small number of pellets examined were composed of the hair of the various mammals and contained also small bones and the wing-cases of beetles which could, however, not be identified. There were also leathery " skins " containing numerous seeds, and these I regard as the stomach walls and contents of the voles, etc. The dispersal of seeds by being transported on the feet of birds has often been stressed, but it seems that birds of prey (and other birds feeding on seed-eating animals) may act as even more efficient transporters when they eject in pellets the seeds which their prey has not digested. The only question which I have not the knowledge to decide is whether the seeds once inside the vole are still capable of germination. I put some of the seeds into a pot and one of them germinated within a short time. The pot was unfortunately lost later. The germination of one seed only does not, of course, provide sufficient proof from which to draw conclusions.   O. E. HÖHN.

But, for the Kestrel, feeding at a bird table must be the ultimate in indignity:

Kestrel feeding at bird table.— Recent notes by A. A. Bell and others and by Dr. J. S. Ash (*Brit. Birds*, 58: 469-470) have described several instances of Kestrels *Falco tinnunculus* feeding on carrion. According to *The Handbook*, this is exceptional. The following behaviour may be even more so. All the observations are my own.

During the winters of 1964/65 and 1965/66 a male Kestrel, presumably always the same individual, made irregular visits to a bird table in Edinburgh. The table is situated about 30 feet from a manor house standing in five acres of wild garden near the Queen's Park and within the city boundary. These visits to the bird table, which lasted up to ten minutes and so provided good opportunities for close observation, were confined to cold spells when food was scarce, though Kestrels occasionally catch small mammals and young birds in the garden at other times of the year.

On one occasion in January 1965 the Kestrel landed on the table and was seen to eat broken dog biscuits and also to tear at frozen cooked brussels sprouts though it is doubtful if these were actually swallowed. Another notable instance was in November 1965 when the Kestrel was attracted by uncooked bacon rinds; one of these fell to the ground while he was feeding on it whereupon he picked it up in his beak and carried it off.

D. E. BRADLEY

[It seems of particular interest that dog biscuits were eaten. Frederick E. Warburton (*Auk*, 69: 85) described a comparable case of a female American Kestrel *Falco sparverius* which fed on bread in the grounds of a hospital in Toronto, Canada, on several occasions over five days during hard weather in April 1950. On the first two days this American Kestrel flew down to the bread only after watching Feral Pigeons *Columba livia* eating it.—EDS.]

Man's agricultural activities – particularly ploughing to expose soil, and soil animals otherwise beyond reach – lend themselves readily to exploitation, but by some very unexpected species.

Kestrel persistently following plough and feeding mainly on earthworms Between 28th February and 14th March 1977, while I was ploughing two fields in a semi-intensive arable area near West Tanfield, Ripon, North Yorkshire, an immature male Kestrel *Falco tinnunculus* followed the plough and fed on any sizeable earthworms that were upturned. On many occasions, I saw it very close to the moving tractor, pulling at and eventually eating a recently caught worm. It usually ate its prey on the upturned soil, but sometimes flew off to the nearest tree. The Kestrel fed on all weekdays except one, and for most of the day between 09.00 and 16.00 GMT, so earthworms obviously formed a large part of its diet. *The Handbook* noted that, from an analysis of 80 stomachs by W. E. Collinge, earthworms formed 2.5% of this species' diet. In Nottinghamshire, J. Staton (*Brit. Birds* 36: 245) recorded a Kestrel following a plough for most of the day, but this individual fed on 'field mice' whose nests had been exposed. COLIN SLATER
4 Bridge View Road, Ripon, North Yorkshire HG4 1JM

KESTREL FOLLOWING PLOUGH.

MR. J. STATON recorded (*Brit. Birds*, Vol. xxxvi, p. 245) an instance of a Kestrel (*Falco t. tinnunculus*) which was observed following the plough in October, 1942.

On December 11th, 1945, a ploughman at Frandley, near Gt. Budworth, Cheshire, told me that he had been accompanied all day by a brown bird. It was a foggy day and although the dense mist did not allow the exact nature of its food to be seen, I was able to watch the bird at very close quarters. I found it was a Kestrel and watched it repeatedly fly from a wooden fence surrounding the field to the newly-turned furrows and pick up food of some kind. There was no evidence of field-mice or their nests in the field, as in the instance recorded by Mr. Staton, and so far as I could see the Kestrel was picking up earth-worms and perhaps leather-jackets and other insects. A. W. BOYD.

Mr. A. W. Boyd's observation of a Kestrel (*Falco t. tinnunculus*) following the plough prompts me to record related, though not identical behaviour on the part of a pair of Kestrels in the Gatley district, Cheshire. During the exceptionally cold weather of January, 1940, when 30 degrees of frost were registered locally, the district council was engaged in re-laying the sewer across some fields near my house. A large and powerful mechanical digger was employed, and this turned up the earth to a depth of several feet, well below the frost level. In doing so, a large number of worms and similar creatures were laid bare, and the wake of the digger became a foraging area for many of the half-starved birds of the district. Thrushes, Blackbirds, Redwings, and even a party of seven Stonechats, appeared, but most surprising of all, a pair of Kestrels regularly walked among the smaller birds, picking up worms and centipedes. They made no attempt to interfere with the other birds, but looked thoroughly incongruous. They were quite tame. STUART SMITH.

Buzzards following the plough.—The disease myxomatosis destroyed almost the entire rabbit population of Pembrokeshire during the summer and autumn of 1954 and as rabbits formed the staple diet of the Buzzard (*Buteo buteo*) the following observations may indicate that the Buzzards have been forced to concentrate more on what had previously been their supplementary food.

On four occasions during the spring of 1955 I noticed Buzzards feeding in ploughed fields during actual ploughing operations and they appeared to be picking food from the newly turned soil. There were the usual gulls and crows following very close to the plough, but the Buzzards were keeping at a "safer" distance, usually about 30 yards behind. I spoke to several farmers who had also witnessed this behaviour and one told me that he had had three Buzzards following his plough at the same time in the wake of the gulls and crows. *The Handbook* includes earthworms, insects, beetles and larvae in the list of food of the Buzzard, but, except for one probable earthworm, I was not able to ascertain what food was taken on the above occasions. K. SMITH

Ruffs following a plough with Black-headed Gulls.—On 1st April 1965, on the Inner Ribble Marshes, Lancashire, I watched a party of 28 Ruffs *Philomachus pugnax* following a plough with a flock of Black-headed Gulls *Larus ridibundus*. Like the Black-headed Gulls, the Ruffs were spread out over the freshly-turned area, individual groups of them hovering round the plough and dropping to the ground when suitable food was uncovered.

It is not uncommon for Ruffs to feed on ploughed fields in this part of Lancashire, but I have never previously observed them following a plough. M. GREENHALGH

Black Terns feeding after ploughs With reference to the note by Dr A. D. Brewer (*Brit. Birds*, 62: 282) I should like to make some comments on certain aspects of the feeding behaviour of the Black Tern *Chlidonias niger*. As long ago as 1907 Dr R. M. Anderson (*The Birds of Iowa*: 125) wrote that Black Terns 'evince little fear of man, and large numbers will often follow a man plowing, hovering over his head and looking for grubs turned up by the plow'. On 4th July 1962, in Waukesha county, Wisconsin, U.S.A., I myself saw several Black Terns flying close behind a motor plough, dropping down to pick up what were apparently worms from the furrows; this was only a few hundred yards from a lake where there was a breeding colony with at least 100 adults.

These observations, like Dr Brewer's, relate to the American race of the Black Tern *C. n. surinamensis*; hunting for land insects in the southern United States was also mentioned in 1921 by A. C. Bent (*Life Histories of North American Gulls and Terns*: 296), who referred particularly to their catching the moths of the cotton-boll worm *Heliothis obsoleta*. As long ago as 1840, however, J. A. Naumann (*Naturgeschichte der Vögel Deutschlands*, x: 206) reported that European Black Terns *C. n. niger* occasionally search for earthworms on fallow land many miles from water, and I myself have seen this happening over cornfields around Lübeck Bay and south of Lake Dümmer in north Germany. Such behaviour is scarcely mentioned in modern publications on this species. F. GOETHE

Vogelwarte Helgoland, 2940 Wilhelmshaven-Rüstersiel, West Germany

GREEN WOODPECKER FOLLOWING PLOUGH.

On January 11th, 1945, at Cley, Norfolk, I observed a Green Woodpecker (*Picus viridis pluvius*) in a field which was being ploughed. It was seen to alight in a furrow, and whilst under observation, twice flew further along the furrow then being ploughed and started feeding with the Rooks and gulls, which were present in some numbers. The weather at the time was very mild. K. D. G. MITCHELL.

Kestrel and Grey Heron associating with plough On 29th January 1977, while ploughing on my farm at Easingwold, North Yorkshire, I saw a male Kestrel *Falco tinnunculus* standing on a recently turned furrow and clawing at the soil, presumably in search of invertebrate food; at the approach of my tractor, it flew off. The following day, again while ploughing, a Grey Heron *Ardea cinerea* alighted on freshly turned furrows. When disturbed by the tractor, it flew in an arc and landed about 40 m behind the plough; on being disturbed again, it flew into an adjoining field, but returned about 15 minutes later and appeared to be eating earthworms. Interrupted a third time, it flew away.

R. HOULSTON
Manor Farm, Oulston, Easingwold, North Yorkshire

In the last case, perhaps we should not be too surprised at the Heron following the plough. The Cattle Egret evolved a feeding pattern walking at the feet of African game animals and snapping up the grasshoppers and other large insects disturbed as the game moved through the grass, and found no difficulty in adapting the technique to man's herds of cattle when they replaced the game. As an expanding species, moving into Europe, it, too, met ploughing and the soil animals exposed as the furrows are turned, and now may often be seen in southern Europe following behind tractors with the gulls. That the herons as a family are both versatile in their hunting approach, and astonishingly catholic in their diet, is shown by this series of notes.

Grey Heron hunting by swimming On the evening of 20th September 1973, at the RSPB reserve of Leighton Moss, Lancashire, I saw an adult Grey Heron *Ardea cinerea* fishing near one of the meres. After a while the bird took off and flew low over the water, but at this point my attention was diverted. When I looked again, seconds later, I was surprised to see that it had settled on the mere in deep water. It remained still for a few minutes and then began to swim forward very slowly, with its head and neck stretched out in front close to the water's surface. After swimming for approximately four metres the heron succeeded in catching a large fish resembling a Roach *Rutilus rutilus*. Immediately its prey was secured the bird took off with no apparent difficulty and flew to a nearby island, where it devoured its meal.

J. DRIVER
Hartrigg Farm, Kentmere, Kendal, Cumbria

Grey Herons eating Water Rails On 29th December 1974, Dr R. J. Raines and I were birdwatching at the Dee Marshes, Parkgate, Cheshire, when we noticed a Grey Heron *Ardea cinerea* eating a Water Rail *Rallus aquaticus*. On closer observation of the marshes, we could see Water Rails seeking shelter from the incoming tide on rafts of floating vegetation. Small groups of herons landed nearby, seized rails in their bills and then flew to shallow water, where they

drowned their prey. At one stage, we saw four herons each devouring a rail. Though large concentrations of Water Rails (sometimes hundreds) are a feature of high tides at Parkgate, I know of only one previous instance of this behaviour by Grey Herons. If it continues, however, there may be a sharp decline in the wintering population of Water Rails on these marshes. CHRISTOPHER W. MURPHY

Heron eating House Sparrows.—Seton Gordon's recent note and the accompanying editorial comment on Herons *Ardea cinerea* eating birds (*Brit. Birds,* 59: 37) prompt me to record similar feeding behaviour by a captive Heron which came into my possession as a juvenile in December 1963. Although unable to fly, it is quite healthy and has the free run of my garden at Fareham, Hampshire.

On numerous occasions during 1964-66 this Heron has captured and eaten House Sparrows *Passer domesticus*, apparently juveniles in every case and many of them ones which have only just left the nest. The capture has always been accompanied by noisy mobbing from other sparrows in the vicinity, but this stops when the victim is either eaten or dead (in a few cases the corpses have been left uneaten) and at all other times the sparrows ignore the Heron completely. The prey is usually stalked slowly and then captured with a lightning stab as soon as it is within range, but occasionally when a sparrow is out in the open the Heron rushes at it and snatches it up before it realises the danger. The dead sparrows are always dipped in water before being swallowed.

These observations suggest that Herons may take birds more frequently than has been supposed, although it would be unwise to generalise from a captive individual. This Heron is otherwise fed on fish and it seems at least possible that the feathers from the sparrows may aid pellet formation. Other prey taken by it include Slow-worms *Anguis fragilis*, Common Lizards *Lacerta vipera*, House Mice *Mus musculus*, beetles, flies, moths, woodlice, earthworms and bread.

R. E. Jones

[The main points of interest here seem to be the methods of capture (especially the dashing at young birds in the open as an alternative to stalking them) and the negative reactions of the other House Sparrows to the Heron unless it actually has a live young sparrow. This contrasts with their behaviour towards such predators as Jays *Garrulus glandarius* and cats.—Eds.]

HERON SWALLOWING SNAKE.

On May 26th, 1928, a friend and I were walking along a " drove " on the Somerset peat moors when our attention was directed to a Heron (*Ardea c. cinerea*) standing in the grass of a meadow which abutted on the drove ; it was easy to see that the bird was engaged with something in the grass, and a moment or two later its head was thrown up in the air with a grass snake quite two feet long dangling from its bill : with two or three gulps the bird swallowed the snake whole. Eels occur here in the larger rhines but are usually small. I mention this, as any suggestion of the creature being an eel may be dismissed, as we were too close to the bird to allow the possibility of such a mistake, and partly hidden by alder bushes we were stationary before the bird's head was raised. Stanley Lewis.

Immature Heron disgorging large eel On 6th March 1971 W. Martin-Hurst found an immature Heron *Ardea cinerea* lying on its back in a meadow by the River Usk at Llansantffraed, Breconshire. It was gasping for breath and unable to stand up. He carried it about a mile to his home at Scethrog whereupon the bird suddenly disgorged, tail-first, a large eel weighing exactly one pound and measuring $25\frac{1}{2}$ inches in length, with a maximum diameter of $1\frac{1}{2}$ inches. The Heron, without the eel, weighed 3 lb 9 oz. After resting for a short time in a covered box the Heron became aggressive when approached, and on being released flew off strongly. E. Bartlett *Ty'n-y-Caeau, Brecon*

Eels are among the normal diet of this species, but the above incident is remarkable for the size of the eel and its effect on the bird. *The Handbook* (3 : 129) included a Grass Snake *Natrix natrix* two feet long in a list of recorded food items of the Heron. Eds

Herons must sometimes share their marshland habitat with others:

Tawny Owls feeding young on fish.—In April 1963 I found the nest of a pair of Tawny Owls *Strix aluco* in an old oak at Penderyn, Breconshire. It contained two eggs, one of which hatched on 30th April and the other on 1st May. On 9th/10th May I spent the first of a number of nights in a hide which I had erected at the nest for photography; the female Tawny Owl brooded the young continuously and the cock paid four visits. On the 14th/15th I found that there was now only one chick. On the 18th/19th the female was still brooding the single chick while the male brought food, but at 4 a.m. she left the nest for about 20 minutes and returned with a very large Brown Rat *Rattus norvegicus*, the head and body of which alone must have been ten or twelve inches long; this meal lasted ten minutes and in the morning all that remained was the head.

It was on 25th/26th May that I first saw the male Tawny Owl come back with a small fish and he brought a second before midnight; soon after 4 a.m. the female returned with a Blackbird *Turdus merula*. On the 29th/30th the male twice brought a fish to the nest and one of these was a small Trout *Salmo trutta* which I was able to photograph as the young bird held it in its bill; the female paid only one visit that night, with what seemed to be a Field Vole *Microtus agrestis*. On 1st/2nd June both adults brought fish, the male two and the female one: plate 25 shows the male arriving at the nest with a Miller's Thumb *Cottus gobio*.

The fact that I saw no less than seven fish brought to the nest shows that this pair of Tawny Owls, and particularly the male, were taking this prey quite regularly, although, apart from Brown Rats, Field Voles and two Blackbirds, I also recorded shrews *Sorex spp.*, Moles *Talpa europaea*, a House Sparrow *Passer domesticus* and a Meadow Pipit *Anthus pratensis* and so they were evidently quite catholic in their diet. The fish were probably from a stream about half a mile away. *The Handbook* does refer to Tawny Owls taking fish, but this may well be the first time that it has been photographed. KERI WILLIAMS

Carrion Crows submerging to catch fish In early June 1973 I witnessed a pair of Carrion Crows *Corvus corone* plunging into the River Severn at Shrewsbury, Salop, to catch fish. One crow jumped feet first from a concrete ledge into the water and remained totally immersed for a few seconds before reappearing with a fish in its bill. The second crow received the captured fish and dashed it several times on the ledge. The dead fish was then taken to some young crows perched on the roof of a nearby building. The whole operation lasted about 20 minutes and was repeated several times, each time successfully. The crows took turns in the fishing and killing operations. JOHN HUGHES

There are many instances of Carrion Crows taking fish and other food from water, for example *Brit. Birds*, 40: 158, 245; 41: 278; 44: 323; 49: 91, but this observation is exceptional. The success rate was high even for terns *Sterna* or kingfishers (Alcedinidae) while the fact that two crows should have learned to plunge right under water is very remarkable. EDS

Obviously Kingfishers would be expected in such surroundings, although not tackling such large prey. Blackbirds, too, it would appear!

KINGFISHER SWALLOWING A FROG.

I HAD no idea that Kingfishers (*Alcedo i. ispida*) ate frogs, but Mr. Topp, taxidermist of Reading, very kindly sends me the following particulars —" The other day a Kingfisher was sent in from Theale and I found on opening the bird a large frog, it must have killed it, I cannot think how he could have swallowed such a large one, the hind leg of the frog was 2½ in. long."   HEATLEY NOBLE.

Blackbird taking frog.—On 10th June 1953 I was surprised to see a Blackbird (*Turdus merula*) carrying a large frog in my garden at Birkenhead, Ches. The bird alighted, and proceeded to peck at the frog about the abdomen and legs. I rushed at the bird in an attempt to scare it off, so that I could examine the prey, but it flew off carrying the frog by one leg. I am aware that small frogs are known as prey of the Blackbird, but this was a full-sized specimen which must have measured at least 2 inches long in the body.

R. J. RAINES

Birds' adaptability can be seen at its best in feeding associations. A simple example of this is the rapid accumulation of hordes of vultures round the abandoned kill of a lion, benefitting from the leftovers. Feeding associations need not be restricted to birds picking up the scraps behind predators or after an accident, and they may involve very different types of both bird and food!

Common and Black-headed Gulls feeding on road corpses With reference to the note by P. K. Kinnear (*Brit. Birds* 71: 80), I should perhaps record that, shortly after the publication of my paper on 'Feeding habitats and food of Black-headed and Common Gulls' (*Bird Study* 19: 173-186), Dr J. I. Meikle wrote to me pointing out that, during 1971 and 1972, he had, for the first time, noted Black-headed Gulls *Larus ridibundus* feeding on the carcases of mammalian road casualties around Galashiels in southwest Scotland. Hares *Lepus* and hedgehogs *Erinaceus europaeus*, as well as the more frequent rabbits *Oryctolagus cuniculus*, were eaten. As P. K. Kinnear pointed out, this food source was not mentioned in my paper, but I have noted Black-headed Gulls feeding on rabbit carcases on two occasions in Scotland in recent years. Common Gulls *L. canus* are known to feed on animal carrion on the shoreline, so perhaps it is less surprising that they have taken to feeding on mammal corpses on roadsides, particularly in summer, when their natural foods may be scarce. J. D. R. VERNON
55 Wolfridge Ride, Alveston, Bristol BS12 2PR

Blackbird feeding in association with Mole.—On 13th June 1967, by one of the ponds in South Gardens, Harting, Sussex, I saw an adult female Blackbird *Turdus merula* following the trail of a Mole *Talpa europaea* which was tunnelling just under the surface of the soft water-side soil. As the squirming vein of loose earth wormed its way along, the Blackbird moved with it and picked up any food that became exposed. A second female Blackbird approached, but was immediately driven away by the original one which then resumed her position at the head of the burrow. This seems to have been an interesting case of opportunism in the face of an unexpected source of food. G. R. GERVIS

[Robins *Erithacus rubecula* have also been seen attending on Moles as they work (see David Lack, 1965, *The Life of the Robin*: 132).—EDS.]

Kittiwakes associating with feeding Razorbills The feeding association with Razorbills *Alca torda* noted by R. E. Scott (*Brit. Birds*, 65: 259) is not confined to Little Gulls *Larus minutus*, since on 3rd July 1972 I recorded similar behaviour involving Kittiwakes *Rissa tridactyla* at Ilfracombe, Devon. A note in my records reads: 'Two Kittiwakes feeding near three Razorbills offshore seemed to be dropping down near where the auks were diving and plunging head and neck below the surface, perhaps feeding on small fish or animals disturbed by the auks. They later settled when the Razor-bills stopped diving, but rose to follow them when they moved away.' I too saw the Kittiwakes diving down at the Razorbills, which then submerged, but I could not decide whether this was a deliberate attempt on the part of the gulls to make the auks dive, or whether the latter instinctively dived when the gulls swooped down towards them to pick from the sea where they had surfaced. The group was later joined by two Herring Gulls *L. argentatus* which similarly fed in the area, both settling on the sea and dropping down in flight, but these made no attempt to dive towards the auks.

The time was 18.15 hours BST and the sea quite rough, whipped up by a force 4 south to south-west wind.   W. E. JONES
Ford House, Northfield Road, Ilfracombe, Devon

Feeding association between Common Tern and Razorbill
On 8th September 1974, at Ferrybridge, Dorset, we watched a feeding association involving a Razorbill *Alca torda* and an adult Common Tern *Sterna hirundo*. The latter was accompanied by an immature Common Tern and an immature Arctic Tern *S. paradisaea*. The Razorbill was feeding in the Fleet very close to Chesil Beach, permitting views down to five metres. The terns, which were in a loose group, kept pace with the Razorbill which could be observed as it swam submerged in the clear, shallow water. The adult Common Tern closely watched the Razorbill's progress and as it surfaced persistently dived just in front of the auk to catch fish driven to the surface. In about 20 minutes it was seen to feed only when the Razorbill surfaced, suggesting that this action was deliberate. The two immature terns were feeding normally and did not exploit the opportunities provided by the Razorbill.

J. CANTELO and P. A. GREGORY
52 Lower Mortimer Road, Woolston, Southampton SO2 7HF

Associations of this type are perhaps to be expected in areas where food is plentiful and space allows many birds to use the same site. It is hardly surprising that a similar situation should occur on fresh water.

Spotted Redshanks associating with surface-feeding ducks On 28th February 1976, at the wildfowl reserve on the Isle of Grain, Kent, I watched some 40 Shoveler *Anas clypeata* and ten Mallard *A. platyrhynchos* dabbling and upending, respectively, as a close group. Gradually, 20 Spotted Redshanks *Tringa erythropus* waded in and joined them, immersing their heads and mandibles while swimming in the muddy water. This behaviour, which I watched for at least ten minutes, resembled that recorded by O. J. Merne (*Brit. Birds* 62: 495). During autumn 1975, parties of up to 40 Spotted Redshanks had frequently been observed feeding in close groups, but this was the first time that I recorded any association with other species. The only comparable reference I have found is by J. F. Reynolds, involving a Marsh Sandpiper *T. stagnatilis* and two Hottentot Teal *A. hottentata* (*Brit. Birds* 67: 477); others relate to feeding associations between Marsh Sandpipers and other species in shallow water (*Brit. Birds* 68: 294, 295).

T. E. Bowley
210 Avery Way, Allhallows, Rochester, Kent

It is interesting that this opportunism is exploited only occasionally: rarely do the notes imply that a chance feeding association has become a habit.

Baillon's Crake feeding in wake of Water Rail

The several notes on feeding associations between various species in both Britain and Africa (*Brit. Birds* 68: 293-297) reminded me of an observation of similar behaviour. On 6th October 1973, near Palaeochora, Crete, I had brief views of a Baillon's Crake *Porzana pusilla* feeding secretively in dense vegetation along the muddy margins of a small river mouth. During 7th-9th October, it was joined by a Water Rail *Rallus aquaticus*, which fed more openly, in rather deeper water outside the vegetation. With the arrival of the rail, the Baillon's Crake became bolder and fed almost exclusively in the other's company, following it closely. I watched both birds at very short ranges and could see material being stirred up by the actions of the Water Rail, caught by the water current and brought to the surface. The Baillon's Crake picked actively at this debris, staying 30-80 cm behind the Water Rail as it moved along the water's edge. In three days of fairly close observation, I saw it feed only in this manner.

John Parrott
Zoology Department, Tillydrone Avenue, Aberdeen AB9 2TN

In most of these cases, the relationship can be seen to be beneficial to one species without being detrimental to the other, a situation outside the normal definitions of either commensalism or symbiosis, in which some form of mutual benefit exists. Occasionally, feeding associations can be difficult to explain:

Dartford Warbler associating with Stonechat On two occasions in mid November 1976, at the Grasslands Research Institute farm at Hurley, Berkshire, we observed a Dartford Warbler *Sylvia undata* apparently associating with a male Stonechat *Saxicola torquata* in a field of red clover *Trifolium pratense* overgrown with sow-thistles *Sonchus*. It spent much time foraging among the thistles, frequently near the ground but often quite conspicuously in the upper foliage, and once among the bare branches of a hawthorn *Crataegus monogyna*. If the Stonechat had moved off while it was feeding, the warbler would perch on a thistle head, call and look round, apparently trying to locate the chat. Once it had succeeded, it would fly directly to it and the two would usually then perch conspicuously side by side on adjacent thistle heads. The Dartford Warbler normally resumed feeding close to the Stonechat, but also made several sorties of up to 70 m.   J. TALLOWIN and R. E. YOUNGMAN
Grasslands Research Institute, Hurley, Maidenhead, Berkshire
53 Seymour Park Road, Marlow, Buckinghamshire SL7 3ER

C. J. Bibby has commented: 'The same curious relationship is frequent in Dorset, as described by Dr N. W. Moore (*Brit. Birds* 68: 196-202) and observed on numerous occasions by myself. Although the two species frequently occur in the same places, they are unlikely to compete for food because of gross differences in their hunting methods and the locations of their food items. I can only propose that the skulking Dartford Warbler takes advantage of the vigilance of the Stonechat, which has a good view from its feeding perches, is decidedly wary and is noisy when alarmed.' EDS

From feeding associations, it is only a short step for one species to take to more persistent harassment and snatching of food items caught by its unfortunate 'victim'. The borderline between an association and out-and-out parasitism may not always be distinct.

Black-headed Gulls associating with feeding Goldeneyes On 24th December 1974, at Bartley Green Reservoir, Warwickshire, I noticed that a Black-headed Gull *Larus ridibundus* was always in close attendance on a male Goldeneye *Bucephala clangula*. This association was confirmed at the reservoir on 2nd January 1975, when three female Goldeneyes were involved, each with its attendant Black-headed Gull. The ducks were diving repeatedly, and each time one surfaced the appropriate gull would fly to join it. The feeling that this was a deliberate behaviour pattern was enhanced when two of the Goldeneyes flew to the other end of the reservoir to be followed immediately by their attendant gulls. As soon as the Goldeneyes resumed diving, the Black-headed Gulls consistently repeated their previous behaviour.

The Handbook (5: 64) mentioned that the Black-headed Gull 'frequently snatches food from . . . diving ducks, grebes and coots'. In this instance, however, no intimidation was observed, and the behaviour would seem to be more similar to the feeding association observed between Black-headed Gulls and Shoveler *Anas clypeata* by E. C. Gatenby (*Brit. Birds*, 61: 31) and, perhaps more appropriately, to those between Little Gulls *L. minutus* and Razorbills *Alca torda* noted by S. G. Madge (*Brit. Birds*, 58: 192) and R. E. Scott (*Brit. Birds*, 65: 259). One can only assume that the turbulence created by the diving Goldeneye was sufficient to disturb and bring to the surface organisms and submerged material on which the Black-headed Gulls were feeding.   A. J. GERRARD

PARASITISM OF BLACK-HEADED GULLS.

THE Tufted Duck (*Nyroca fuligula*) on a large reservoir near London feed at fairly regular hours during the day-time, and as soon as they begin parties of Black-headed Gulls (*Larus ridibundus*) at once resort to it. They have established a definite parasitic relationship with the duck, and this is the method. A bird dives and a Gull (sometimes a pair) at once flies over to its neighbourhood and settles on the water. As soon as the duck reappears, the Gull flies up from the water, hovers a yard or so above the duck's head, and then (quite gently) drops down upon it. The duck dives again, and nine times out of ten drops the food, the Gull half submerging to recover it before it sinks. What the ducks were feeding upon I could not make sure, but it was neither fish nor weed—probably *Ancylus, Limna* and other molluscs. All the Gulls on the water (there were thirty-five among ninety-seven ducks) pursued this method ; the stoop was obviously made with the intention of flustering the duck, and the stratagem was nearly always successful. I have noticed an amateurish parasitism among Lesser Black-backed Gulls (*Larus fuscus*) and Black-headed Gulls pursue Lapwings, but this manœuvre was orderly, professional and precisely executed. In no ornithological works I have read have I seen mention of this interesting relation. H. J. MASSINGHAM.

The birds of prey, so often regarded as paragons of avian nobility and virtue in popular literature, have developed parasitism to a high degree, perhaps demeaning themselves in the process but doubtless surviving the better for it. In Kenya, I can remember watching a Wahlbergs Eagle, a specialist predator, spend several minutes cautiously unpicking the viciously thorny and bulky nest of a family of Buffalo Weavers to reach the nestlings inside. About fifty metres away, a pair of Tawny Eagles were, apparently, indolently sunning themselves on the crown of a lightning-struck tree. Once the Wahlbergs Eagle had penetrated the nesting chamber and extracted two or three squawking but helpless youngsters, the smaller male Tawny took off and drifted, casually but quickly, across to the baobab containing the Weavers' nest and knocked the much smaller Wahlbergs Eagle off its perch. No sooner had it seen off the Wahlbergs Eagle – which made little protest – and bent over to begin tearing at and devouring the Weaver youngsters, than with a rush of wings its female arrived – and it too was dispossessed. So much for nobility, and so much for the niceties of family life in eagle circles. Such behaviour occurs nearer to home:

Kestrel taking prey from Short-eared Owl On 31st March 1971, at approximately 6.45 p.m., we were watching a Short-eared Owl *Asio flammeus* quartering over dune grassland on Buddon Ness, Angus. On its second stoop the owl caught a small mammal and rose high in the air carrying its prey in one foot. The victim was probably a Short-tailed Vole *Microtus agrestis:* this species was known to be present and, indeed, the remains of one were found in a pellet that same evening. Two Carrion Crows *Corvus corone corone* began to harry the owl which by then had risen to a considerable height. After a minute or two of this, a Kestrel *Falco tinnunculus* emerged from a pine wood near-by and flew at the owl on what appeared to be a collision course. The latter dropped its prey which fell past the attendant crows and was deftly caught by the Kestrel in flight. The whole sequence of events at this stage was so rapid that we were unable to determine the sex of the Kestrel before it returned to the cover of the wood.

Kestrels in this area appear to be opportunist feeders: in 1969 one was flushed from the corpse of an oiled Guillemot *Uria aalge* not far from the site of the above incident, and in January 1971 one was seen hovering over beehives and later perched on the alighting board of a hive.   T. M. CLEGG and D. S. HENDERSON
City Museum and Art Gallery, Albert Square, Dundee DD1 1DA

Kestrel taking prey from Barn Owl.—On the afternoon of 10th February 1968, not far from Loch Arthur, Kirkcudbrightshire, J. N. Dymond, A. MacIver, Mr. and Mrs. J. McLaurin, G. L. A. Patrick, M. Rogers and I watched a Barn Owl *Tyto alba* hunting over some rough pasture. We saw it catch a Short-tailed Vole *Microtus agrestis* which it carried into a barn near-by. It soon reappeared with a second Barn Owl and we watched the latter drop into a patch of *Juncus* to emerge with what was almost certainly another Short-tailed Vole. This owl also seemed to be making for the barn with its prey, but a Kestrel *Falco tinnunculus*—which until now had been sitting motionless on some wires, apart from two brief and apparently fruitless journeys to the ground—suddenly stooped at it with shrill calls. As the Kestrel passed below the Barn Owl, only 25 yards from us, it rolled on its back and seized the vole in both talons. The owl was flapping along about four feet above the ground and for a few seconds it flew on, losing height, carrying the vole and the upside-down Kestrel with one foot. Then the wildly flapping Kestrel broke loose with the vole and flew off. Both Barn Owls disappeared shortly afterwards, but we later saw the Kestrel feeding perched on a dead tree about 150 yards away.   M. J. EVERETT

Food piracy by Kestrel There have been several notes concerning one predator robbing another (e.g. *Brit. Birds* 64: 317-318; 66: 227). On 11th May 1975, I was watching a male Sparrowhawk *Accipiter nisus* flying over marshland at Berrow, Somerset, carrying a small mammal. Suddenly, a Kestrel *Falco tinnunculus* rose up from nearby dunes and vigorously attacked the Sparrowhawk, forcing it to release its prey. The Kestrel then dropped down to the marsh, retrieved the mammal and flew off.

BRIAN E. SLADE
40 Church House Road, Berrow, Burnham-on-Sea, Somerset TA8 2NQ

Food piracy by Red-footed Falcons On 1st July 1975, I was watching up to 15 Red-footed Falcons *Falco vespertinus* hunting on the Tadten Plain, near Andau, Austria, with about six Kestrels *F. tinnunculus*, two Buzzards *Buteo buteo*, two Montagu's Harriers *Circus pygargus* and a Marsh Harrier *C. aeruginosus*. About 20 m from me a female Kestrel dropped on to what appeared to be a small rodent. Having secured her quarry, she flew some 5 or 6 m, landed in the field again and mantled the prey. Suddenly, a male Red-footed Falcon flew low across the field and approached the Kestrel

from behind; on landing, he struck the Kestrel a blow, knocking her over. A scuffle ensued and the Kestrel made off without her prey, which the Red-footed Falcon secured and, having flown some 40 m and settled, began to devour.

J. K. R. Melrose (*in litt.*) has informed me that on 20th September 1971, in the Danube Delta, Romania, he observed a female Red-footed Falcon take prey from a Kestrel in flight, by swooping in at the latter's talons. RAYMOND H. HOGG

Schoolhouse, Crosshill, Maybole, Ayrshire KA19 7RH

Derek Goodwin comments that he has seen Red-footed Falcons in Libya and south France feeding by robbing Lesser Kestrels *F. naumanni* of prey. EDS

Piratical Short-eared Owl On 17th November 1974, at Needs Oar, Hampshire, on an area of rough grassland, I was watching a Stoat *Mustela erminea* which was carrying a small mammal. Suddenly a Short-eared Owl *Asio flammeus* appeared and dived at the Stoat, which dropped its prey. The Stoat stood on its hind feet and retaliated but the owl snatched up the prey in its talons and flew off. C. R. WOOD

6 Laurel Close, St Leonards, near Ringwood, Hampshire

In these last two notes, the theme is more normal but the overtone of bravery persists:

SHORT-EARED OWL TAKING STOAT.

ON October 1st, 1947, on Fremington Marsh, North Devon, I flushed a Short-eared Owl (*Asio f. flammeus*) from the still warm body of a female Stoat (*Mustela erminea*). The Stoat had deep claw cuts on its back and deep wounds over the eyes and on the neck. The Stoat is not recorded in *The Handbook* as being a normal prey of the Short-eared Owl. GEOFFREY H. GUSH.

Blackbird eating slow-worm's tail In very warm, dry conditions at 10.30 GMT on 24th June 1976, in my father's garden at West Cross, Swansea, West Glamorgan, I watched a male Blackbird *Turdus merula* at a distance of about 2 m struggling with a slow-worm *Anguis fragilis* on a stone path. It passed the slow-worm, which was about 20-25 cm long, several times through its mandibles, but the reptile finally escaped down a deep crevice in the stonework. At this point, the Blackbird noticed the 4-5 cm shed tail section of the slow-worm, which was still moving a short distance away; it seized it, passed it through its mandibles and then ate it whole. R. J. FOOTE

⇨ 3 ⇦

Physique

Birds are masters of the air: only bats and a few gliding mammals and reptiles can compete with them in this element. This mastery, and the mobility it gives, has, among other things, opened for birds the possibilities of migration (p97), allowing them to exploit seasonal food sources that other animals cannot reach in time. Flight, though, demands considerable specialisation and sophistication. One impact of the development of wings is the loss of hands, leading to the wide range of adaptations to be seen in birds' beaks and feet to offset this disadvantage. Another is the need for structural reallocation – a bird's body is compact and its bones specially light to keep its centre of gravity close to the axis of its wings and allow effortless balance. In flight, head and neck are counterbalanced by tail, and, if need be, by the legs too. Birds also have a highly developed musculature and respiratory system and their blood supply is often judged superior to anything found in mammals.

Against this background, it is hardly surprising that various aspects of avian physique have been popular topics for bird watchers' observations, studies and comments. In 1923, long after the era when the 'horseless carriage' was preceded by a man with a red flag, *British Birds* carried a series of notes of bird flight speeds measured on car speedometers (with some accuracy) and by timing progress over calculated distances (with rather less nearness to the truth on some occasions!). Note the attention to physical detail given by Dr Joy.

VELOCITY OF FLIGHT AMONG BIRDS.

To the Editors of BRITISH BIRDS.

SIRS,—In reference to the correspondence on the flight of birds and the respective speed of different species (Vol. XV., p. 298), it may be of interest to record that of *Chætura nudipes* and *Chætura cochinchinensis*. Both these species have a normal flighting speed of something very nearly approaching 200 miles an hour, enormously in excess of the powers of any other bird with which I am acquainted. In North Cachar, Assam, these birds used to fly directly over my bungalow in Haflang, flying thence in a straight line to a ridge of hills exactly two miles away and when over the ridge at once dipping out of sight. We constantly timed these Swifts and found that stop watches made them cover this distance in from 36 seconds to 42 seconds, *i.e.* at a rate of exactly 200 miles an hour to 171.4. Green Pigeons took about 2 minutes 30 seconds to 2.45 seconds, Paroquets 2.15 seconds to 2.30 seconds, but were more difficult to time as they did not fly in so direct a line. E. C. STUART BAKER.

SIRS,—I have had an opportunity to ascertain the exact speed of the flight of a bird. I was in a car going along a rather narrow road when a Willow-Warbler (*Phylloscopus trochilus*) flew out of a hedge. It flew along over a ditch at the side of the road for about 15 yards, going at exactly the same speed as the car. I looked at the speedometer, and it recorded 23½ miles per hour. The speedometer is certainly correct as it is a nearly new high-class car. There was a light wind behind us. The bird cannot have been affected by the air pressure being altered by the car as it flew just opposite the driver's seat, where I was, but not driving. It was, of course, frightened by the car, so it was not necessarily the rate of its migratory flight; it also altered its course once or twice, as if to dart into the hedge, but it did not drop back more than a few inches in doing this. It would be interesting if some other correspondents were able to time birds under similar conditions. NORMAN H. JOY.
SONNING, NR. READING, *May 5th*, 1922.

[The possibility of deriving some information as to the speed at which certain birds fly by means of the method described by Dr. Norman Joy, occurred to me some years ago, and I made a few observations while being driven in a friend's car. Since then I have always driven myself and after one or two attempts I gave up trying to make observations as I found that it was impossible to do so with any degree of accuracy and to drive at the same time. A year or two later there was a letter on the same subject in the *Field*, but I do not remember reading of any other observations of the kind. My records were made in the autumn of 1906 and were briefly as follows :—

House-Sparrows kept just ahead of the car over a distance of about 200 yards when we were going 24 m.p.h., and were slowly caught up and passed at 29 m.p.h.

Starlings kept well ahead of the car, gaining a little, at 24 m.p.h.

A Pied Wagtail kept ahead at 21 m.p.h.

An adult cock Blackbird kept ahead at 22 m.p.h.

A young cock Blackbird kept ahead at 18 m.p.h.

In each case the birds rose in front of the car and kept ahead of it, except the Sparrows that were overtaken, so that they could not have been affected by the wind of the car. To have any real value a large number of observations would of course be necessary for each species. N. F. TICEHURST.]

This note provoked a series of replies and subsequent issues added to the list of species on record.

VELOCITY OF FLIGHT IN BIRDS.

SIRS,—A few days ago I timed a Cormorant (*Phalacrocorax carbo*) for sixty seconds flying a straight course along the Orwell estuary. During this period it covered a distance of three-quarters of a mile as nearly as I could estimate by careful calculation from the one-inch ordnance map. This was at the rate of forty-five miles per hour. The light wind slightly favoured it. The flight was obviously of a normal, unhurried character.   T. G. POWELL.

IPSWICH, *April 22nd*, 1923.

VELOCITY OF FLIGHT IN BIRDS.
To the Editors of BRITISH BIRDS.

SIRS,—On May 21st, 1924, I timed a pair of Yellow Buntings (*Emberiza c. citrinella*) flying in front of my car for about 150 yards. The speed registered on the speedometer was 22 miles per hour. This was at Locksley, near Stratford-on-Avon.

The following day I also timed a cock Blackbird near Wellington his speed being, for about 50 or 60 yards, 26 miles per hour.

THOS. L. S. DOOLY.

FLIGHT SPEED OF GUILLEMOTS, RAZORBILLS AND PUFFINS.

DURING speed trials of a ship in the neighbourhood of Ailsa Craig in May, 1937, I observed that Puffins, Razorbills and Guillemots (*Fratercula arctica, Alca torda* and *Uria aalge*) with beam or following winds were all easily able to pass the ship steaming at approximately 37 land miles per hour. Upon one occasion with the ship steaming at that speed into a direct head wind of 10 land miles per hour a flight of Guillemots came up from astern and were able to pass the ship, though slowly ; overtaking speed, calculated on time taken to pass the total length of the ship, estimated at 3 land miles per hour, giving them a total speed of 50 land miles per hour through the air.   H. R. H. VAUGHAN.

As early as 1916 and 1917, observers writing under pseudonyms (doubtless indicating their involvement with the Royal Flying Corps but endeavouring to conceal the fact during the War) had commented on the height at which birds fly.

HEIGHT AT WHICH BIRDS FLY.—In an interesting letter in the *Field* (4.12.'15, p. 936), signed " Tinnunculus," it is stated that " while flying on duty between Bethune and La Bassée at a height of 8500 ft. this afternoon (Nov. 26) I was astonished to see a flock of about 500 ducks, or geese, passing over Bethune at least 3000 ft. above the level of our machine. The wind was about 45-50 m.p.h. N.N.E. and the birds were travelling due south."

HEIGHT AT WHICH BIRDS FLY.—" An Observer " writes (*Field*, 20.1.17, p. 113) that when flying in France in the middle of August, at about 9500 ft., he saw a large flock of birds high above him and with the aid of binoculars he identified them as " Swallows."

Writing in 1943, Flying Officer Carr-Lewty summarised his own observations; of these, the Curlew was subsequently endorsed.

One does not usually see a bird above 300 feet or 400 feet above ground level except flocks on migration, but I have occasionally noted various species at surprising altitudes, amongst these, Pink-footed Geese (*Anser f. brachyrhynchus*) at 7,000 feet ; Mallard (*Anas platyrhyncha*), 6,300 feet ; Curlew (*Numenius arquata*), 4,600 feet ; Swan, 3,850 feet ; Swift, (*Apus apus*), 3,400 feet ; Wood-Pigeon (*Columba palumbus*), 3,100 feet ; Golden Plover (*Pluvialis apricaria*), 3,000 feet ; Starling (*Sturnus vulgaris*), Rook and Swallow (*Hirundo rustica*), above 2,000 feet. I have never seen birds above cloud even when it has consisted of a thin layer about 100 feet thick and only 300-400 feet above ground level. They appear· to prefer, in daylight at least, to remain within sight of the ground.

Curlews at 4,500 feet.—On 29th July 1955 Pilot-Officer A. L. Carey, R.A.F., on a flight over Northamptonshire, flew into a flock of about six Curlews (*Numenius arquata*) at 4,500 feet. One of the birds was later found impaled on the aircraft. The wind was from the N.E., at 10 knots, and the birds were flying above a 1,000 feet layer of strato-cumulus whose ceiling was 3,000 feet. There are few observations of waders flying at such a height, so that isolated records like this seem worth noting.

C. DOUGLAS DEANE

[In his paper on "Aircraft observations of birds in flight" (*antea*, pp. 59-70), Capt. K. D. G. Mitchell is able to give only two personal records of waders flying at over 4,000 feet. Both referred to parties of Lapwings (*Vanellus vanellus*), at heights of 4,200 feet and 6,000 feet. On the other hand, Col. R. Meinertzhagen (*Ibis*, 1920, pp. 923-924) quotes a record of a Green Sandpiper (*Tringa ochropus*) flying at 12,000 feet; and fourteen cases of Lapwings between 2,000 and 8,500 feet, the majority between 5.000 and 6,000 feet.—EDS.]

But this pales into insignificance before the swan, recorded first of all as an echo on a radar screen, and only identified positively by the pilot of an aircraft.

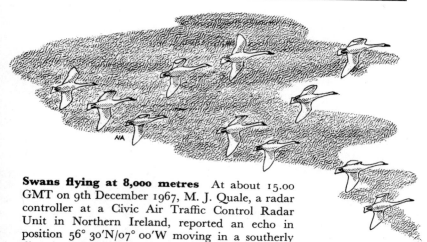

Swans flying at 8,000 metres At about 15.00 GMT on 9th December 1967, M. J. Quale, a radar controller at a Civic Air Traffic Control Radar Unit in Northern Ireland, reported an echo in position 56° 30'N/07° 00'W moving in a southerly direction at a ground speed of about 75 knots. He verified that there were no meteorological balloons in the area, so presumed that the echo came from a flock of birds. A height finder gave a reading of 26,000-28,000 feet (about 8,000-8,500 m), which seemed very high for birds. MJQ asked the pilot of a civilian transport aircraft due to land at Prestwick Airport, Strathclyde, to make a slight course deviation while descending to pass near the suspected flock of birds; passing within 1.6 km, the pilot reported 'a flock of about 30 swans [*Cygnus*]', at just over 27,000 feet (8,200 m). MJQ had the flock in sight as a radar echo until it disappeared about 27 km from Lough Foyle, Co. Londonderry, probably having descended below the cover of the radar.

A height of 8,200 m seems to be the highest so far recorded for any species of bird over the UK. Captain K. D. G. Mitchell (*Brit. Birds* 48: 59-70) published some of his sightings of birds over Europe from the cockpits of piston-engined aircraft at much lower levels; with the modern jet aircraft and much-improved radar, more such reports are now possible and should be encouraged.　　　　A. G. STEWART

31 St Andrew's Avenue, Prestwick KA9 2DY

The question of height has a particular relevance to two structurally similar but technically unrelated birds, the House Martin and the Swift. Of these the House Martin is less studied and remains the more enigmatic.

High flight of House Martins In his book *The Palaearctic-African Bird Migration Systems* (1972), the late R. E. Moreau estimated that possibly 90 million House Martins *Delichon urbica* winter in Africa. He mentioned how very infrequently these birds had been observed there and discussed the idea put forward by R. Verheyen in 1952 (*Gerfaut*, 42: 92-124), that they spend much of their time too high

to be seen, suggesting that there must be a change in their habits between summer and winter.

I maintain that there is no sudden change and that House Martins also probably spend a good deal of their time at great heights in their Palearctic breeding quarters. Particularly during fine weather in August and September, I have often seen them flying at heights where they are only just visible with 8 × 30 binoculars. The technique I use is to relax in a deck chair and look up into the sky with good sunglasses in order to pick out a high-flying group of martins. If binoculars are then focused on these birds, searching the sky at greater distances beyond them often reveals more. One might call this 'sky watching' and it is exciting to pick out these birds and watch them in flight at heights where they are quite invisible with the naked eye. It appears that they can gain height quite quickly, possibly on rising thermals. In Africa the opportunity for this must be vastly greater than in the Palearctic region.

House Martins often return to roost well after sunset and later than most other birds. This would also help to explain their elusiveness in their African winter quarters.   D. D. Lees

Hailey Lodge, Hertford Heath, Hertford

High flight of House Martins D. D. Lees (*Brit. Birds*, 68: 216-217) claims that House Martins *Delichon urbica* 'spend a good deal of their time at great heights in their Palearctic breeding quarters'. In his book *Bird-Watching and Bird Behaviour* (1930), the late Sir Julian Huxley described going out early one morning in the Upper Thames valley in the hope of seeing something of the courtship of the House Martin. 'To my surprise, there were no martins to be seen—none in or by their nests, none flying round. I walked round the place, and up and down the towpath, along which spread a faint mist from the river, and still I saw nothing of my birds. Then from the barn came a single swallow, and flew steeply up into the sky. I followed its flight with my eyes and suddenly saw why I had failed to find the martins. They were all up there in the blue, circling round in company with some barn-swallows and chimney-swifts, from which I could just distinguish them at the height they were flying. The sun had not yet risen where I stood on the solid earth; but he already reached the birds high above my head. . . . There can be little doubt that when I first came out, half an hour before I saw the birds, they had already flown up to greet the sun and make themselves a longer day; but how far above the earth they flew before they reached the light and began to circle in it and sink with it, I do not know.'

These observations must raise the question whether House Martins, like Swifts *Apus apus*, roost on the wing; for they are very rarely found at roost, except when incubating or brooding in the nest.   E. J. M. BUXTON
Cole Park, Malmesbury, Wiltshire

In one way, the Swift has also retained its ability to puzzle observers.

WING-STROKES OF THE SWIFT.

WITH reference to the question that has been raised as to the movement of the wings of the Swift (*Apus a. apus*), whilst watching the flight of these birds at Aix-les-Bains this summer my wife and I distinctly saw a Swift flying away from us towards a dark blue mountain (the Mont du Chat) in the sunshine, and the wings caught the sun first on one side and then on the other as they were raised. This seems to be good and positive proof that these birds do raise their wings alternately.   WALTER CAVE.

WING-STROKES OF THE SWIFT.

WITH reference to the note (*antea*, p. 60) as to whether Swifts (*Apus a. apus*) raise their wings alternately in flight, I remarked this fact as long ago as 1911, and both my brother, Brian Stoneham, and I often refer to it. At first I thought it was an optical illusion, but whilst in Mesopotamia in 1918 and 1919, I had wonderful opportunities of observing many thousands of these birds, among others, on migration often flying about 6 feet from the ground, and was able to settle, without a matter of doubt that on occasion the Swift does fly "alternately." Again this year, when Swifts are so numerous everywhere, I have seen it happen on several occasions with certainty, and many other times on which it was difficult to decide definitely. Mr. Cave is the first person to my knowledge who has published this observation, but I have many notes and private records of the same.

H. F. STONEHAM.

To this day, there are many bird watchers who find it difficult to be certain that the Swift does not, at least occasionally, use its wings in a way that in swimming would be described as the 'crawl' rather than the 'butterfly' stroke.

HOW LATE DO SWIFTS STAY OUT AT NIGHT?

IN 1924 I have had some experience with Swifts (*Apus a. apus*) slightly similar to that which Mr. Hamilton had in 1923 (Vol. XVII., p. 110). I ringed fifty Swifts, all but seven in nests in the thatch of cottages near Tisbury, Wilts. On July 30th, 1924, I thoroughly searched the thatch at one side of a cottage and ringed two young and one adult. The next evening at 10 p.m., a dark night, I examined all the nests again, taking an hour over it. I ringed nine young Swifts and found again the two with rings on, but did not find a single adult. I was fortunately able to see clearly that they were all young, as I had the strong electric lamp of a car close by. I did not see an adult leave a nest, nor was one reported to me by several bystanders. Three or four of the young birds flew out directly I put them back in the nests. Not liking this I took four of them home and put them in a cupboard for the night, and let them go in the morning, three miles away.

It is quite evident that the adults were still out, as I feel sure that they would have been in their nests with their young, and not over the top of a ceiling, where they might have got to in two places. Of course I felt in as far as I could in these places.

While on the subject of Swifts, is it known where they roost in South Africa and Madagascar (*Prac. Handb.*, II., p. 7)? It also makes one wonder where they roost on migration, because, of course, they have to have very special places for roosting. Do they roost with Alpine Swifts (*A. m. melba*) in North Africa? Do they fly night and day for several days? A physical impossibility one would think, but is it? Their wonderful flight is done with very slight strokes of the wings, and after all in nature examples of nearly perpetual muscular motion do occur. Leaving out the heart beat, etc., does not this occur in a fish in a swift running stream ? It has to keep its fins constantly on the move and nearly its whole body working its tail, even when hiding behind a rock, as here it has to contend with the back current.   NORMAN H. JOY.

" NIGHT SOARING OF SWIFTS."
To the Editor of BRITISH BIRDS.

SIRS,—I quite agree with Mr. James J. Cash (*antea*, p. 88) that Swifts (*Apus a. apus*) do return to their nesting and roosting quarters after their occasional high vesper flights. About thirty years ago, on several occasions, I investigated this matter, and recorded my observations in *The Naturalist* so long ago as 1907 (p. 113) and I have several times confirmed them since. I was favourably situated for watching a particular colony, and on certain clear bright evenings (usually in June) when I saw the birds (males, I believe them to be) mounting in large circles just before dusk, I would take up my stand on a hill that stood behind the buildings in which several pairs nested and roosted. I used a pair of "sea and night" binoculars which were very good for evening work, or even for light nights. I watched the birds as long as possible, and never saw any signs of descent. But as soon as they were completely lost to view I made my way quickly to just below, where they nested, a matter of only a few minutes. In about a quarter of an hour later I could distinctly hear the flutterings of the returning birds above me in the darkness, and sometimes a bird appeared to have a little difficulty in finding its exact quarters. Although they appeared to return singly, yet there was but little time between the first flutter and the last. I have since noticed that such evenings when Swifts take these curious vesper flights are followed by dark nights. Occasionally at that season of the year we have a night or two when it does not really get dark at all, or not until after 1 or 2 a.m., when I have given up the hunt. On several such evenings I have turned out to observe Swifts and certain bats. But the Swifts went to bed, and the bats stayed at home !   H. B. BOOTH. BEN RHYDDING, YORKS.

Dr David Lack's studies of the Oxford University Swifts, and some magnificent time-lapse film of radar screens covering the London area taken by Marconi Ltd., seem to have settled this issue beyond doubt. At dusk, Swifts emerge for their evening feeding, rise to a great height and may move as far as the Wash in search of suitable insect concentrations for feeding. Swifts are certainly the most aerial of British birds, feeding, roosting, even mating on the wing. Amazing though it seems, it is likely that once it has fledged, the nestling Swift may not put its feet on the ground (or, rather, a wall or roof cavity) for two or three years and countless thousands of flying miles to, from and around Africa.

Many water birds exist in a dual element. In Penguins, the 'secondary' of these – the sea – has assumed dominance, and the wings, in the process of evolution, have become rigid flippers so that Penguins are now flightless. Our own auks are at a halfway stage: poor flyers, but very competent under water. The sea ducks are one stage less aquatic: Seton Gordon opens the account.

PERIODS OF DIVES
MADE BY LONG-TAILED DUCKS.

THE following notes on the diving of the Long-tailed Duck (*Clangula hyemalis*) were made at Bamburgh, on the Northumberland coast. I saw nothing of these ducks during the severe weather of November 1919, but during December they were numerous just off-shore, especially on calm days (which are extremely rare) with a heavy swell on the rocks, for this probably stirs up their food.

On one occasion, December 16th, I timed a drake during six dives, as follows : 37, 37, 37, 30, 37, 37 seconds. As will be seen, his periods of submersion were extremely regular. On December 18th I watched for some time a pair diving energetically. The drake kept under longer than the duck, half a dozen of his dives being as follows : 37, 42, 36, 35, 33, 32 seconds, and those of the duck, 33, 37, 35, 33, 33, 32 seconds. On emerging, the duck seemed to shoot up more buoyantly than the drake. In the afternoon I timed the drake for four dives, as follows : 42, 40, 42, 45 seconds. The periods during which the birds were above water between the dives I timed as follows : 10, 8, 6, 8, 7, 11 seconds. On December 21st I timed a pair diving and emerging almost simultaneously, as follows : 34, 32, 37, 38, 40, 43, 36 seconds. Before the two longest of these dives, the birds swam for some time on the surface of the water.   SETON GORDON.

PERIODS OF DIVES
MADE BY LONG-TAILED DUCKS.

I HAVE read with much interest Mr. Gordon's note on the periods of dives made by the Long-tailed Duck (*antea*, p. 244). A female of the above species remained on Bardowie Loch the first week in November 1919. I timed this bird's dives fairly often during the period it was here and found that it usually remained under water about 65 seconds, but never less. The longest dive that I noted was 70 seconds. This bird rested for about a couple of minutes between each dive. The depth of water where the duck usually dived was about 35 feet.

J. ALASTAIR ANDERSON.

There is an appropriate comment on the relevance of depth to the time spent under water.

PERIODS OF DIVES
IN RELATION TO DEPTH OF WATER.

Mr. J. Alastair Anderson's note on the diving of the Long-tailed Duck (*antea*, p. 298) supports what I believe is a general rule for the periods of dives made by diving birds. The rule is a simple one, namely, twenty seconds for the first fathom and ten seconds for every fathom thereafter. The conditions are that the birds are actually going to the bottom, that they are not disturbed or alarmed in any way, and that the times of not less than three consecutive dives are used in reaching an average. The depth recorded by Mr. Anderson is 35 feet, or $5\frac{5}{6}$ fathoms, and the times 65 to 70 seconds, which agrees very closely with the rule. I have discovered an important exception to the rule. When a bird is travelling along the bottom and crosses a reef at right angles to its course, the period of the dive does not correspond to the general depth of the bottom, but to the general depth *plus* the height of the reef. Thus, a bird is diving in three fathoms of water and crosses a reef one fathom in height. The probable time of the dive will not be 40 seconds (according to the rule), but 40 seconds *plus* 10 seconds=50 seconds, the reef having an effect on the period of the dive, as if it increased the depth to an extent equivalent to its height above the bottom.

Great practical difficulties attend the recording at the same time of the periods of the dives and the depth of the water. Since I began to collect records, I have been forced to the conclusion that the only practicable way of obtaining the depth, without disturbing the birds, is the indirect one of determining the position of the bird on the water in relation to fixed points. The method is not free from liability to error, and on sea-water the chances of making mistakes are increased by the rise and fall of the tide. Hence, it would appear that the problem is one for as many observers as possible, working independently and maintaining a critical attitude towards their results. Since 1910 I have collected the times of over three thousand dives made by nineteen species of Auks, Grebes, Divers, Cormorants, and diving Ducks. Such is the regularity of these birds when they are working in a given depth of water, that I am convinced there is always a constant and narrow relation between the period of the dive and the depth to which the bird descends ; though, that this relation is correctly expressed by the rule I have given above, I am not yet prepared to affirm, in view of the liability to error in the method of observation.

J. M. Dewar.

The Long-tailed Duck seems to be an ideal subject, illustrated by these two detailed studies well worth presenting in full.

THE DIVING HABITS OF THE LONG-TAILED DUCK.

DURING the last five years, we have had one or two excellent opportunities for observing at close quarters the diving habits of the Long-tailed Duck (*Clangula hyemalis*).

On November 4th, 1928, two were watched on the Llwyn-on Reservoir, Brecknockshire. They were, as far as we could see, a male and female in first winter plumage.

It was a dull morning with a slight rain falling, and the birds were well out from the shore. At first sight their appearance on the water conveyed to us the distinct impression of enlarged editions of the Little Grebe (*Podiceps r. ruficollis*) in first winter plumage, but it was the manner in which they dived which made identification certain, for one of them, diving with its tail towards us, displayed the characteristic diving habit of this species, open wings and spread tail, so that from behind, the observer sees, as the bird disappears under water, two long, pointed wing-tips with the wide-spread tail between. This habit was one of the things that impressed us most when we saw our first specimen in October, 1923, and it has also been noted and described by Mr. Chas. Oldham (*antea*, p. 215).

The birds seemed to remain under water for such a considerable length of time that we decided to time a few of their dives, which we did with two watches, and were surprised to find that four consecutive dives gave 63, 65, 53, and 63 seconds, respectively.

This reservoir is approximately 70 feet deep at the deepest point, and while we cannot say exactly in what depth they were diving, it was certainly in water at least 30 feet deep.

On comparing these figures with published records we find that the *Practical Handbook* says : " duration of dive usually from 30–40 seconds (C. E. Alford)," and T. A. Coward in his *Birds of the British Isles* writes : " The duration of dives has been estimated at over forty seconds, but birds I have watched hardly remained so long."

Other notes are published in *British Birds*, Vol. XIII., where on page 244 Seton Gordon records dives of from 30–45 seconds, and on page 298 J. Alastair Anderson notes a bird making dives of from 60–70 seconds in 35 feet of water. Chas. Oldham (*antea*, p. 215) records dives of from 30–46 seconds.

We have recently had a further opportunity of timing a series of dives under most favourable conditions. A female, apparently in first winter plumage, appeared on the Lisvane Reservoir, near Cardiff, on November 25th, 1928, but the weather was so stormy on that day, and the water so extraordinarily rough, it was impossible to keep the bird in sight sufficiently long for accurate observations to be made ; but a week later, December 2nd, the bird was still there, and a dead calm and bright, sunny morning, enabled us to mark the exact second of its disappearance and reappearance. Twelve consecutive dives were timed, and the duration of these were 54, 54, 53, 53, 55, 59, 60, 58, 56, 61, 53 and 59 seconds respectively, giving an average of 56¼ seconds.

It would therefore appear that this species, when diving in deep, fresh water, frequently stays under for periods of from fifty to sixty, and sometimes seventy, seconds.

Dr. J. M. Dewar, in an article in *British Birds*, Vol. XIII., pages 315 and 316, suggests that a simple general rule for computing the depth of water from the duration of a bird's dives is to allow " twenty seconds for the first fathom and ten seconds for every fathom thereafter." Applying this rule to our observed average above, 56¼ seconds, the depth works out to 27¾ feet.

We have, by the kindness of Mr. Neil J. Peters, M.Inst.C.E., the Cardiff City Water Engineer, been able to consult a large scale (50 feet to 1 inch) chart of Lisvane Reservoir, which shows the bottom contours at 2 feet intervals, and by plotting out upon it the birds' position, by means of observations made while it was diving, we find that the spot indicated lies between the 26 and 28 feet contour lines, and that the charted depth agrees approximately with that arrived at by Dewar's 20–10 second rule. Geoffrey C. S. Ingram.
H. Morrey Salmon.

With regard to Mr. Oldham's quotation from Dr. Townsend, that Long-tailed Ducks (*Clangula hyemalis*) use their wings under water (*antea*, p. 215), I might add that, when alarmed by the sentry duck (always a female), the drakes actually emerge from the water in full flight as if they had flown from the depths. This happens only on the sea in Orkney, where they are very wild, but not so on the inland waters of Loch Stenness, where they are just as tame and usually allow a sailing boat to approach within a few yards of them. I have never seen Eiders or Velvet-Scoters emerge thus in full flight from the sea. H. W. Robinson.

LONG-TAILED DUCKS IN HERTFORDSHIRE AND THEIR DIVING HABITS.

On November 1st, 1928, and again on the 2nd, 4th and 5th, I saw two immature Long-tailed Ducks (*Clangula hyemalis*) at Tring. This species is known to have occurred at Tring on five previous occasions in the last forty years. Of these, four were in November and the fifth within three days of the beginning of that month. The evidence is perhaps insufficient to argue a regular movement at this season, but such punctuality suggests something more than mere coincidence.

On November 1st the two birds were on the same reservoir, diving incessantly during the half-hour that I spent with them. On the 4th, when I was at the reservoirs with Mr. Bertram Lloyd, the larger bird, which I took to be a male, had moved to an adjoining reservoir, where its isolation enabled us accurately to time its dives. Two series of seven consecutive dives gave an average of 34.3 seconds below and 7.9 above water (35:6, 34:8, 30:7, 31:5, 35:8, 38:5, 30:9 and 38:7, 36:10, 31:8, 33:11, 34:9, 39:8, 36:9), *i.e.*, 81.3 per cent. of the time was spent below. On the 5th a series of eight and another of nine gave rather different results (38:8, 39:7, 42:7, 40:15, 43:8, 39:7, 38:25, 40:7 and 32:14, 30:26, 39:15, 41:10, 40:9, 45:12, 46:9, 42:14, 41:8), an average of 40 seconds below and 11.8 above, *i.e.*, the bird was below the surface for 77 per cent. of the total time.

Most, perhaps all, diving ducks, when intent on feeding, swim lower in the water than when at rest and the tail is then awash and slightly expanded. In some, *e.g.*, Tufted Duck, Pochard, Scaup and Red-crested Pochard, no further expansion takes place when the bird dives, but in others, *e.g.*, Common Scoter, Goldeneye and Smew, the tail-feathers are distinctly fanned as the bird goes down. In the Long-tailed Duck this pectination is much more apparent than in any other species I know, and the individual feathers stand out like the fingers of an outspread hand. But more remarkable is the way in which the bird half opens its wings in the act of diving, just as a Guillemot does, a habit it shares with the Harlequin (J. G. Millais, quoting W. H. St. Quintin, *Brit. Diving Ducks*, I., p. 141) and, according to Dr. C. W. Townsend (*Auk*, XXVI., p. 240), with Eiders and Scoters too. Personally I have never remarked this habit in either Eider or Scoter. Most diving ducks, *e.g.*, Tufted Duck and Pochard, as may be seen in the London parks on any winter day, go down and swim below water with wings pressed close to the body. Dr. Townsend (*loc. cit.*) asserts that Long-tail, Harlequin, Scoters and Eiders use their wings for propulsion under water, and it may be that opening the wings in the act of diving is correlated with that action. CHAS. OLDHAM.

Most other diving birds show broad similarity, the grebes perhaps briefer under water, the Shag rather longer, with one spectacular endurance record.

Duration of dives of Black-necked Grebes.—*The Handbook* gives the recorded lengths of dives of Black-necked Grebes (*Podiceps nigricollis*) as ranging from 9 to 50 seconds and adds "but about 25-35 seems most usual". At King George VI Reservoir, Staines, Middlesex, on 15th September 1959, two different birds were each timed on six consecutive dives, these being spread over a period of 10-15 minutes. The respective figures were 55, 55, 52, 54, 57 and 50 seconds and 58, 59, 65, 68, 37 and 64 seconds. Thus only two of twelve dives were within the range given in *The Handbook*. The birds were not travelling across the reservoir and so it seems safe to assume that they were searching for food which must have been either far below the surface or very scarce.   RICHARD CARDEN

PERIOD OF DIVES OF GREAT CRESTED GREBE AND POCHARD.

WITH reference to Mr. G. Bolam's note (*antea*, p. 189) on the diving of the Great Crested Grebe (*Podiceps c. cristatus*) the following observations may be of interest. They were made upon a bird which spent the morning of January 8th, 1921, in short periods of alternate diving and preening on an open piece of water, close to a main road, from which its movements could easily be watched. The dives were not made through fear and were consequently not as long as those made by a bird wishing to escape detection. During periods of five and three minutes it made nine and six dives respectively, and the times spent under water were 20, 25, 12, 17, 12, 20, 22, 25, 25 seconds and 20, 12, 25, 20, 18, 18 seconds. A Pochard (*Nyroca f. ferina*) was also timed during five minutes and it too made nine dives in that period, of 10, 20, 25, 16, 13, 10, 30, 20 and 20 seconds' duration.   W. P. G. TAYLOR.

Duration of dives of Black-throated Diver.—In Sutherland on 25th May 1955 we were able to make continuous observations for nearly four hours on the diving of a Black-throated Diver (*Gavia arctica*). The site was a loch half a mile wide and seven miles long. The bird, one of a pair, was first seen at 12.45 p.m. as it made its way up the loch by a series of long dives. Our subsequent observations were then made in an area about half a mile square, which was fed by two substantial mountain streams. Here the bird began diving repeatedly, presumably for food, and after some 15 minutes we began to record the duration of both dives and rests. We continued this for 3 hours 25 minutes until at 4.35 p.m. the diver was finally lost to view in rough water. During this period there were 201 dives and only three relatively long periods of rest—of 1½, 8 and 7 minutes respectively.

The Handbook quotes the maximum diving times recorded for this species by four observers and these vary from 43 seconds to 2 minutes. The last was when a bird was travelling a distance of a quarter of a mile and we suggest that the duration of dives greatly depends on whether the bird is feeding or travelling. During our observations the longest single dive was 63 seconds, the shortest 5 seconds and almost half (96 out of 201) were between 48 and 50 seconds. The rests were mostly of 10-18 seconds. Consecutive dives of 50 seconds and over were always followed by a series of dives of under 40 seconds and rests of over 18 seconds.   In all, 2 hours 17 minutes 33 seconds were spent underwater for 1 hour 8 minutes 25 seconds on the surface. The three long rests were not spread evenly over the period.   In the short rests the bird often dipped its bill in the water, shook its head, stretched its neck and gave an occasional cry.   In the long rests it also preened feathers of breast, back and rump for anything up to two or three minutes.   IRENE A. JOYCE and ALAN E. JOYCE

DIVE OF THE GREAT NORTHERN DIVER.

ON three occasions in May, 1923, I timed the dives of Great Northern Divers (*Colymbus immer*) in St. Mary's Harbour, the Isles of Scilly.   Late in the evening of May 5th, with a calm sea, the dives were most regular, being nearly all as near as possible 40 seconds up and 20 seconds down, the maximum down being 52 seconds, all of these being when he was unsuccessful.   When a capture was made the times were irregular of course, being from 29 to 31 seconds down.   The catch appeared to be small cuttle-fish.   He, and another just outside the harbour, were still fishing when darkness compelled me to give up watching them.

On the night of May 7th, with a choppy sea, one in the harbour was down as nearly as possible 40 seconds, but his stays on the surface were only from 10 to 15 seconds.   Twice he was below 47 and 45 seconds respectively.   He caught nothing and was still fishing at dark.

On the morning of May 21st, there was a good deal of ripple on the surface, and a lot of traffic in the harbour.   His dives averaged 34 seconds and his periods on the surface only 9 seconds.   I watched him for nearly an hour and he caught nothing at all during this period.   The birds were in full summer plumage.   H. W. ROBINSON.

DIVING OF THE SHAG.

ON September 5th, 1937, about noon, we watched an adult Shag (*Phalacrocorax a. aristotelis*) diving off the north-east corner of Skokholm Island. The bird was in the lee of the island where the sea was moderate, and was diving in several fathoms of water. We observed the bird leave the rocks and watched every dive until it returned.

In all it dived 54 times, and we measured the duration of each dive, and in 35 instances the length of time spent on the surface. The average duration of a dive was about 53 seconds and between each dive the bird spent 21 seconds on the surface (average). Three dives lasted 10 seconds or under, thirteen lasted over 1 minute. Of these by far the most remarkable was one of 170 seconds. The next longest were of 85 seconds and 70 seconds. It appears that the length of time spent on the surface bears little relation to the length of the dive, for after the dive of 85 seconds the bird spent only 15 seconds on the surface, whereas after a dive of 48 seconds it spent 33 seconds on the surface. It should be remarked, that the longest time spent on the surface (37 seconds) was after the exceptionally long dive already noted.

On about three occasions the bird was seen to rise to the surface with a fish in its beak, which it swallowed. Once it had an eel with which it struggled for some time, but which escaped. On this occasion the bird was on the surface for 35 seconds.

Of the 54 dives, 45 were made with " the graceful curving leap out of the water " remarked by Coward. The other 9 were made in the manner of a Cormorant—the bird slid quietly under the water.

After the fifty-fourth dive the bird washed, ducking head, neck and back under the water, and splashing with the wings. Several times before it had washed its beak, and once was seen to drink.

It is possible that during the long dive of 170 seconds the bird put its head up unobserved to breathe, but certainly the bird did not rise fully to the surface as after every other dive. There was no boat, nor any other human being within sight to alarm it. Coward timed the dives of the Great Northern Diver at 2 and 3 minutes, and on one occasion a bird " timed for a quarter of an hour was out of sight for 14½ minutes, only remaining on the surface for a second or two at a time ". It seems therefore by no means impossible that the dive of 170 seconds recorded by us was made without any rise to the surface.

E. J. M. BUXTON,
R. S. HARKNESS.

With some ingenuity, it is even possible to estimate progress under water:

RATE OF PROGRESS OF GREAT CRESTED GREBE UNDER WATER.

IT is not often that opportunity offers for the accurate computation of the rate at which a diving bird progresses under water ; the following note may, therefore, be of interest.

During a sojourn in Lincolnshire in October 1920 I came upon a Great Crested Grebe (*Podiceps c. cristatus*) in the river Glen, where that stream flows straight and sluggish as a canal through the fen country, enclosed by high embankments on either flank, and destitute of weeds or obstruction on the surface as far as the eye can reach. There was no difficulty in getting right on top of the bird, so to speak, nor in following it as far as one listed. This I did for about half an hour, timing the dives by watch and stepping the distance (and I think I may claim to be able to count yards very accurately in that way), and I was surprised at the very slight variation that occurred either in the length of dive or the time it occupied. The bird was followed in either direction it chose to take, and twenty dives did not vary more than three yards in length, nor four seconds in duration ; the mean being 77 yards and 58 seconds. I quite expected that both speed and distance covered would have been greater. The bird, I may add, was an adult, and, though naturally doing its best all the time, it showed little signs of fatigue when I left it, and was very rarely at all flurried. It was never noticed to open its wings under water, nor did it once forbear to raise its whole body to the surface, even when it was forced to come up within a few yards of me. For the most part I walked along the top of the bank, some 30 feet above the water, but occasionally descended to the water's edge to get the Grebe at closer quarters. GEORGE BOLAM.

The fishing success of the Kingfisher depends on a relatively short period under water, and on the impetus and accuracy of the dive itself. One way of gaining extra impetus is to start from a higher perch.

High diving by Kingfisher Miss K. M. Hollick reported a Kingfisher *Alcedo atthis* diving 4.8 m from a wall into a brook (*Brit. Birds* 66 : 280-281). During cold weather on 18th December 1976, near Newton Solney, Derbyshire, M. E. Taylor and I saw a Kingfisher perched on an electricity cable which passed at about 11 m over the River Trent. It was watching the water intently and, after about four minutes, dived steeply into the shallows about 1 m from the bank and caught a fish; it ate its catch on a stone on the bank, returned to the cable and resumed its watchful position. R. A. FROST

In some circumstances, this extra impetus may well be necessary:

Kingfisher diving through ice to catch fish On 15th January 1977, from the hide at Birdholme Wildfowl Reserve, near Chesterfield, Derbyshire, several friends and I saw a Kingfisher *Alcedo atthis* settle on the top of a willow *Salix* about 3 m high. The water in front of the hide, about 17 m² in extent, was free of ice, but the rest of the 1.6-ha lake was frozen over and lightly covered with snow. We anticipated that the Kingfisher would take a fish from the open water, as it had done many times before; but it suddenly dived from the top of the willow straight through the snow-covered ice some 9 m from the front of the hide and disappeared under the ice; after about one second, it emerged from the very small entry hole with a fish about 6½ cm long and returned to the willow bush.

PHILIP SHOOTER
153 Market Street, Clay Cross, Chesterfield, Derbyshire

The question 'Why don't woodpeckers get fearful headaches when drumming?' would have been answered in the early days of *British Birds* with the sharp reproof that the sound is produced *vocally*, and not mechanically – so the chance of a headache is nil. Not until the early 1930s was the suggestion commonly made that the noise was literally caused by the drumming of the beak on an appropriately resonating (and often dead) branch.

" DRUMMING " PERIOD OF LESSER SPOTTED WOODPECKER.

THE following observations on a pair of Lesser Spotted Woodpeckers (*Dryobates m. comminutus*) were made by myself in my Rectory garden in Gloucestershire in 1931. The birds bred somewhere near at hand, though I did not locate the nesting hole, but these notes refer chiefly to the " drumming " period, and the noise was produced most frequently quite early in the morning, often commencing soon after sunrise. It was first heard on February 14th from a poplar tree, but all other observations recorded here were from a horse-chestnut tree, fortunately growing near my bedroom window. I watched the birds through strong field-glasses, and until the leaves appeared every movement of the birds while " drumming " could be followed with great ease, and the very rapid strokes of the bill against the wood, which produces the sound, could be clearly made out. By far the most used " drumming " station was on the horse-chestnut, and always within an inch or two of the same spot, and *both* sexes produced the noise. All the following remarks apply to the horse-chestnut :—

Heard early in morning, March 23rd. Began to " drum " regularly on April 6th and kept it up most mornings until May 1st. The " drumming " then ceased. On June 23rd parent birds feeding young out of the nest were seen about the garden. Early on July 7th " drumming " began again from the same tree and apparently from the same spot as before, but leaves obscured the vision. This was kept up until July 30th, when it ceased. On October 26th at 7.5 a.m., on a very cold, frosty morning, the female bird started to " drum " on *exactly* the same spot as in the spring, and kept it up for about eight minutes. Suddenly a male Great Spotted Woodpecker settled on the " drumming " branch, drove the smaller bird away, and began hacking with his bill (not " drumming ") on the exact spot used by the smaller birds. This he did for perhaps one minute. No " drumming " was heard in the year later than this.   F. L. BLATHWAYT.

Even this apparently cut-and-dried account produced a speedy response from a conservative observer, who, in turn, was challenged by Mr Butler.

" DRUMMING " OF GREAT SPOTTED WOODPECKER.
To the Editors of BRITISH BIRDS.

SIRS,—I find it impossible to accept Mr. M. A. Swann's note in the May number (Vol. XXV., p. 364) as a reliable observation.

The drumming of Woodpeckers has always interested me, and I have followed up, located, and watched the performers not once or twice, but perhaps hundreds of times.

That the sound is produced by a very rapid succession of blows of the bill on a branch selected for being in that springy and resonant stage of deadness which precedes actual rottenness is absolutely certain, and this has been confirmed by such a multitude of observers that I should have thought the fact was now established beyond controversy.

Besides our Great and Lesser Spotted Woodpeckers, both of which are common here, and may be watched drumming any day in spring or early summer (a Lesser Spotted Woodpecker has a drumming station on a dying oak within twenty yards of my bedroom window), very many other Woodpeckers, palæarctic and tropical, have the same habit, and I have watched more species drumming than I can remember. Among these I recollect two in particular—*Thriponax hodgii* (Blyth), the great scarlet-headed, black Woodpecker of the Andaman Islands, which drums on the tall, dead " Gurjon " trees scattered through the jungles, and produces an extraordinarily powerful jarring rattle, audible a mile away, and, the last tropical species I have had the opportunity of watching, *Celeus elegans* (Mull.), on dead trees in the forests of Trinidad—another powerful drummer. I know of no case in which birds which produce a certain sound mechanically can produce the same sound vocally also. Personally, I feel sure that Mr. Swann, and others who claim to have observed Woodpeckers of any species drumming without striking upon wood, *have simply had their glasses on the wrong bird, and not the performer*, which was probably clinging motionless and unobserved to another branch between drummings. The mistake might easily be made, as the sudden vibrating rattle is often not easy to locate exactly. A. L. BUTLER.

" DRUMMING " OF GREAT SPOTTED WOODPECKER.
To the Editors of BRITISH BIRDS.

SIRS,—The following note may be of interest to those who are reminded, by the note in the April number, of the old controversy over the " drumming " of Woodpeckers.

Several mornings lately I have heard the drumming of Woodpeckers at Brownsover (near Rugby) and, on March 25th, 1932, I watched a Great Spotted Woodpecker (*Dryobates m. anglicus*) for about fifteen minutes producing this sound. The bird was pecking the trunk of a holly, but usually left off in order to " drum", either turning its head to one side or throwing its head back so that its beak was vertical. Once only did it " drum " while pecking, and then it hammered the wood at one frequency and drummed at about twice the speed.

This Woodpecker, at least, was producing the sound vocally.
M. A. SWANN.

The ingenious Norman Pullen embedded a microphone deep in a suitable branch in 1943, to resolve the question (most elegantly) once and for all.

DRUMMING OF THE GREAT SPOTTED WOODPECKER

BY

N. D. PULLEN.

IN a footnote on p. 284, Vol. ii, *Handbook of British Birds* attention is drawn to the claims made by some writers that the drumming sound produced by woodpeckers is vocal in origin. This claim, in the absence of any direct proof of the contrary merits serious attention, and it was in order to disprove it, if possible, that experiments to be described were carried out.

The arguments for the vocal method appear to be as follows :—

(a) Some observers claim to have heard the sound whilst the bird being watched remained quite still.

(b) More energy than the bird can provide would be required to produce a mechanical noise audible up to a quarter of a mile.

(c) Why, if mechanical, *i.e.* produced by blows with bill, are no indentations or marks to be found at the drumming point.

Against these is the almost overwhelming evidence that rapid vibration of the head and bill occurs whenever the drumming noise is produced; therefore the bill must be hitting the wood or other surface being " drummed."

The conclusion that the bill and the wood make contact is unsound unless supported by direct evidence, other than visual, which at the frequency used is distinctly unreliable. If, for instance the noise was vocal, necessitating for its production rapid movements of the throat muscles, then whilst the mass of observers would still be right regarding the coincidence of movement and noise they would be quite wrong in their conclusion or assumption that the bill must hit the wood at the end of each stroke. It is obvious, therefore, that before other questions can be answered, actual contact must be proved or disproved, and this was done in the early part of 1943. It was decided that if the bird hit the branch then it should be possible to pick up the sound of the tapping by using a suitably constructed microphone inserted in the tree.

For the experiment a microphone was constructed consisting of a stout wooden holder, shaped like a wine glass minus the foot with a sensitive button microphone fixed to the bottom of the bowl and sealed in with a closely fitting lid, the stem of the holder being sufficiently robust to enable it to be fitted firmly into a hole in the tree trunk bored for this purpose. The apparatus was completed by a small battery and transformer, a pair of headphones and about 50 yards of cable. Preliminary tests carried out on a live oak tree showed that small pieces of wood thrown into the tree to a height of 20 feet or so could be heard distinctly hitting the branches as they fell, and on windy days a tinkling sound produced by the smaller branches hitting each other was sufficient to mask any other noise. It should be mentioned that the microphone when sealed

in its container was quite insensitive to air-borne sounds unless the air gap was less than two inches or so. The actual test was carried out on a dead tree situated in a small wood. The drumming point is near the end of a broken bough 25 feet from the ground, the surrounding bushes, etc., providing cover at about 40 yards distance, from which the selected branch could be watched.

The first " drum " was a disappointment, as the bird arrived, drummed and left, before the 'phones had been adjusted ; the second and third attempts were, however, successful. Immediately the head movement began, which could be seen, a rapid tapping sound arrived via the headphones, and at almost the same time could be heard the usual air-borne sound, with this difference : the sound in the 'phones was a series of sharp taps of a rather wooden tone, quite distinct and loud at first, but diminishing in clearness and intensity towards the end. The air-borne sound, being partly muffled by the ear pieces, was less clear, the noticeable part being a distinct but slight pause between the arrival of the 'phone signal and that through the air, the interval, as far as could be judged, being equivalent to about two beats. Drumming lasted for about one second each time, the bird using the same spot or very close to it. An attempt to count the strokes was found to be very difficult, the nearest estimate being 10 to 12 ; it was certainly not as low as 5 nor as high as 20. This result agrees very well with other estimates of 8-10, but more results would be required before any decision could be reached regarding the general use of this frequency.

The first part of the problem could now be considered as solved, definite evidence, other than visual, having been obtained that the bird's bill makes actual contact with the surface. The second part dealing with the particular type of noise produced can be answered if it is shown, as it probably will be, that the frequency of the blows is constant or only varies between small limits. Accepting this as a fact, all the bird has to do is to find a spot on a dead branch or other object where blows struck at its own frequency, *i.e.* about 10, will bring that object into resonance. This theory requires that the tone shall vary according to the type of object struck, *e.g.* wood or metal ; it also limits the bird's choice to a few particular spots. That both of these happen is well known. How the spots are found does not appear to be known. The bird may know that dead branches free from bark are likely or desirable places, but after that it can only proceed by trial and error. No doubt such exploratory work has been observed without the observer's realising its object.

The theory also furnishes an explanation for the absence of marks at the drumming point and the apparent lack of power on the part of the bird. In order to produce vibration of sufficient amplitude to give the desired volume of sound it is only necessary to deliver taps or light blows at the correct rate for a certain time. The bird can therefore afford to expend its energy in maintaining a uniform speed, and provided it can keep it up for the required time the weight of the blows can be very light, certainly much less than would be necessary to damage the surface of the drumming board.

And the headaches? Recent anatomical research has shown that the skulls of some woodpeckers have a pad of shock-absorbent tissue between the base of the beak and the skull itself.

While on the subject of 'drumming', the first volume of *British Birds* was able to offer an editorial note containing an explanation of how the Snipe produces its drumming during display flights. The resolution of this problem, although apparently simpler than the woodpeckers', was just as elegant.

THE " DRUMMING " OF THE SNIPE.

An interesting paper on the " drumming " or " bleating " of the Snipe was read by Mr. P. H. Bahr before the Zoological Society, and is published in the " Proceedings " of that Society for 1907 (pp. 12–35). After discussing the various theories which have been advanced to account for the sound, Mr. Bahr gives excellent proof that in the Common Snipe (*Gallinago cœlestis*), at all events, the " bleat " is produced by the two outer tail-feathers. As the bird makes the downward swoop, the two outer tail-feathers are held widely spread beyond the others—almost at right angles to the body—as may easily be seen with a pair of binoculars, but in addition to this Mr. Bahr states that he can distinctly see these feathers vibrating during the performance of the "bleat." By fixing these feathers to corks and whirling them through the air, Mr. Bahr demonstrated that the sound could be reproduced. There appear to be no special muscles to control the outer tail-feathers, but the muscles at the base of the feathers are sufficiently well developed to perform this function. In structure these feathers differ from the rest of the tail-feathers. The shaft is firm, the outer web narrow with easily separable rami, the inner web extremely broad with long stiff rami firmly held together. It is this latter portion of the feather which produces the sound—the radii, branching from the rami, being firmly interlocked by means of the hamuli and cilia, which are exceptionally well developed. It is, indeed, the great size of the hamuli which furnishes the "essential factor in producing the 'bleat,' in that they hold the stiff rami together like the strings of a harp." In the other tail-feathers the hamuli are fewer and not so well curved, nor so thick. It appears that towards the time of moulting the cilia become worn away and the feathers lose much of their "bleating" power. Mr. Bahr gives June 25th as a late date to hear the "drumming," but I may mention that I have just heard and watched Snipe "bleating" to-day (July 7th) in Hampshire.

In the Jack Snipe (*Gallinago gallinula*) the outer tail-feathers have not this specialized structure, and the author, failing to reproduce the sound, suspects that its production must be accounted for by some other mechanism.

Neither do the feathers of the Great Snipe (*Gallinago major*) produce any sound, and here, too, the rami are soft and easily separable, and the sound produced by the bird, which is of a "snapping" nature, seems to be vocal.

In other Snipe, in which the "bleat" is of varying intensity and pitch, some of the tail-feathers seem to be responsible for the sound. H.F.W.

What of the impact of all this 'high living' (in several senses) on the lifespan of birds? This proved a fertile and fascinating field for assertions and comment in the early days.

THE LONGEVITY OF BIRDS.

IN your review of Mr. H. Eliot Howard's book I notice that you say (*supra*, p. 63) that it is not possible to believe that Wrynecks live for fifty to sixty years. May I ask why? Given that a bird lives in perfectly natural conditions and never suffers from want of food or from excessive cold, what proof have we of the length of its life?

It is well known that a great many birds die on migration, many more die from starvation due to excessive cold and sudden deprivation of food, but of the length of life of such bud and seed-eating birds as Bullfinches, Goldfinches, Yellow Buntings, etc., living in a temperate climate we know but little.

I think one may assume that the life of a pinioned or caged bird would probably be shorter than that of one living under natural conditions, *where its food supply never failed*, and yet the following instances of longevity amongst birds have occurred amongst those in my own collection.

A Barbary Dove which has been in my possession for fifteen years was left me by an old woman who also owned it for fifteen years and who always told me that it was an old bird when it was given to her. It shows no sign of old age unless it be that the innumerable eggs laid by the young hen bird which lives with it are always infertile.

The second case is that of a Chinese Goose which has been in the possession of the family for fifty-seven years.

The third is a Pintail Drake which I bought twenty years ago and which was then an adult bird.

It is well known that Eagles live to a great age. A few years ago we had in our possession the last of the White-tailed Eagles bred in Galloway. The bird was taken from the nest in 1852 and died in 1900. It was chained by the leg to a small hutch and lived forty-eight years under these miserable conditions.

The Wryneck is dependent upon insect food but it leaves us early, and there is no reason why its food supply should fail.

M. BEDFORD.

[The whole subject of the age to which birds live is one about which we are profoundly ignorant and the only positive facts we have concern the ages to which certain captive birds have attained. Of these even we have comparatively few reliable records, and the instances of longevity noted above by the Duchess of Bedford are therefore most welcome. Attention must here be drawn to a valuable article on the subject by Mr. J. H. Gurney, published in the " Ibis " for 1899 (pp. 19-42). In his researches Mr. Gurney found some remarkable records such as a Raven of 69, Parrots of 80, Eagle-Owl of nearly 70, Condor of 52, Eagles of 55 and 56, Heron of 60, Goose of 80, Swan of 70, Collared Dove of 40, and so on, but of the small Passerine and Picarian birds 25 years seems the maximum, and that has only been reached in a very few cases.

We have practically no positive evidence as to the length of life of the wild bird, and I do not think we can argue from instances of longevity in captive birds, which are so kept that the supply of food is unfailing and all enemies and accidents are carefully guarded against. There is perhaps little doubt that members of certain families, such as *Corvidæ*, *Falconidæ*, and *Anatidæ* live longer than birds of other families, but I do not believe that the average life of any species, of which a pair would raise a minimum of say four young each year, can be longer than a few years. If the normal life were much longer, even after taking into account the probable great mortality of the young, I imagine that birds which rear four and more young in a season would literally be swarming in the course of a few years.

Then in the case of a migrant such as the Wryneck, imagine what an individual would have to go through in the course of sixty years : How many miles in all would it journey ? How many storms and fogs might it be expected to encounter at sea ? How many times would it have to steer clear of the fatal lighthouse or lightship ? How many Hawks and Gulls, how many guns and snares would it avoid ? I said that it was impossible to believe that the same birds (*i.e.*, the same pair) lived for fifty or sixty years, but I would say now that I cannot believe that any Wryneck could escape for fifty years the manifold dangers to which it would of necessity be exposed.—H. F. W.]

THE LONGEVITY OF BIRDS.

In reply to your editorial note to my remarks on the longevity of birds, may I say that if they depend mainly upon accident for the curtailment of their lives, the chances are that *a few* survive in a wild state for the natural term of their existence.

I cannot believe that because a bird is saved from starvation and natural enemies its life will be abnormally prolonged under such conditions as caging, pinioning, chaining by the leg, etc., etc.

If, therefore, a bird is known to live thirty to sixty years under these adverse conditions, it looks as though the natural course of its life were a great deal longer than is generally supposed.

So great are the perils of migration, starvation, and their natural enemies that the chances are very much against their surviving for any length of time, and it is in this way that I would suggest that Nature regulates the balance and prevents undue increase.

The fact that one pair of birds apparently returns to the same nesting site (often in a peculiar position) for a great number of years, rather points to the possibility that a very small proportion escapes accidental death. That the same pair *does* return for two or three years I know for a fact, and if they were not the same Wrynecks which returned to the nest for sixty years it would be interesting to know how their numerous progeny decided amongst themselves which of them was to return to the paternal abode, and how they knew that they would find it empty ?

M. BEDFORD.

[It is unfortunate that there is very little basis of recorded fact to go upon in this matter and, therefore, I fear that this discussion tends to become academic. There are so few instances which give us positive proof of the same two individuals returning to the same nesting site that I hope Her Grace will place on record the details of the case referred to above. Reverting to the Wrynecks, I do not think it is necessary to suppose that the young ones came back to the old nesting site ; the suggestion I made on page 63 seems to be the simplest, viz., that it so happened that both birds of the pair never died in any one winter, and that the survivor got a new mate. The individuals might thus have changed many times during the sixty years.—H. F. W.]

APROPOS of your notes on the longevity of birds (p. 79) it it may be of interest to state that there is on the Loch of Skail in Orkney a Whooper Swan which was winged, captured and pinioned sixty-three years ago.

It is well protected on this loch, which is a private one, but it walks about a great deal, often as far as the large tidal loch of Sterness, four miles away. It has met with many accidents in its career, chiefly broken wings, one man in the neighbourhood having set the wing twice in the last six years. Although it has been there so long it is still shy and wild, except when captured after an injury, when it is very savage. What age it really is, it is impossible to say, as it was an adult bird when captured sixty-three years ago.

H. W. ROBINSON.

YOUNG have been raised both this year and last from the mating of a male Barbary Dove, which has been in my possession for twenty-three years, and a young female of the same species.

RICHARD STAPLES-BROWNE.

THE ages to which birds live has always been a subject of interest to me, and the following records from my aviaries may be of value :—
  Lapp Owl, 27 years.
  Ural Owl (a pair), 22 years, and still vigorous.
  Pintail Sand-Grouse, 17 years, and still in perfect
    health, but now lays infertile eggs.
  Wigeon, 20 years.
  Pochard, 22 years (she reared a brood annually for
    20 years).
A wild Turtle-Dove (*Turtur communis*), which was noticeable by reason of its having a stiff leg, turned up about May 1st every year at the place where we fed our water-fowl for twenty-one years.

E. G. B. MEADE-WALDO.

In regard to the longevity of birds, the following translation of a record by the late Herr H. C. Müller in his " Færöernes Fuglefauna " may be of interest :—

" A farmer at Sandhöe took in 1781, during the summer, two young Herring-Gulls out of a nest and reared them at his home. He let them have their freedom, and the Gulls, which appeared both to be cocks, stayed sometimes near the house and sometimes in a field in the neighbourhood, or even made short flights out to sea, from which, however, they always came back. After some years one of the Gulls was accidentally shot during one of these flights ; the other continued its accustomed mode of life, and became so tame that it took food out of its master's hand. Finally, it paired with a wild Gull, and they selected for a nesting place a rocky cliff (near by), from which the cock bird, after the usual time, went back to the farmer's house in company with his mate and half-grown young. During the summer the Gull family lived mostly on the shore, especially when fishing was good, and they then fed chiefly on offal from the fishing, as the entirely wild Gulls do. When the fishing got slack, and particularly during the winter, the pair of Gulls constantly sought food at the peasant's house, and the cock bird still took what was handed to him. . . . In 1846 these remarkably old Gulls were still living, and were consequently sixty-five years old ; but, in spite of this advanced age, carried on under such peculiar relations, there was neither in their colour or in other respects any difference to be detected between them and the entirely wild Gulls. In 1847 the old peasant died, and a short time afterwards the Gulls also went away."

Herr Müller also mentions a Puffin which lived in a peasant's house and yard for twenty-nine years, and finally died as the result of an accident.

C. B. TICEHURST.

LONGEVITY OF SWALLOW.

To the Editors of BRITISH BIRDS.

SIRS,—A few days before Mr. Witherby's article, *The Duration of Life in Birds* (*antea*, p. 71), was published, I was explaining to a friend some of the advantages of bird ringing, among other things, that it would teach us something about this subject. He told me that Miss B. Dowson marked a Swallow (*Hirundo r. rustica*) with a " Canary ring " at West Meon, Hants, some time before the war. It was ringed as an adult, and returned to the same nesting place for nine consecutive years, after which the pair stopped nesting there. NORMAN H. JOY.

78, CRESCENT RD., READING.

As Dr Joy and Mr Witherby suggested it might, ringing has thrown a great deal of light on the lifespan of birds. Even so, the picture is not yet as clear as we would like. The great majority of small birds die during their first or second years, many within a few months of leaving the nest. Those living longer are the exceptions. In larger birds, there are problems with ring wear: certain sea-birds, like the Fulmar, are considerably tougher and more durable than the modern alloy rings placed on their legs! In all cases, birds 'on record' are likely to be exceptions, most wild birds will live for a much shorter time. Nevertheless, ringing has shown that many sea-birds and ducks regularly live in excess of fifteen years, some in excess of twenty. Pride of place goes to a twenty-seven-year-old Arctic Tern; here not just the lifespan is amazing – think of the annual migrations to the Arctic Ocean (p110). Gadding about included, the life distance of this bird must have approached three *million* miles!

→ 4 ←

It is Amazing...

Throughout these pages, observations from hundreds of bird watchers have been collated to demonstrate the extraordinary physical and behavioural adaptability that characterises birds. In many cases, what seems to man to be great prowess in a particular sphere turns out to be quite normal for a bird. However, *British Birds* does receive notes of some of the extremes of bird behaviour, and a selection of these merits a chapter of its own. We start with one of the clumsiest birds on land seeking to achieve apparently impossible heraldic postures – in suitable surroundings:

Cormorants roosting on spire In the late summer and autumn of 1973 Cormorants *Phalacrocorax carbo* regularly roosted on Chichester Cathedral, West Sussex. When this habit was first noted in mid-August only two birds were involved, but numbers gradually increased to a maximum of eight in October and then declined slowly, the last birds being seen at the end of November.

The birds arrived one hour before sunset and took up positions on top of the pinnacles at the base of the spire. After preening, wing-flapping and much fidgeting of the feet they assumed their characteristic upright posture with beaks slightly raised. Thereafter they remained almost motionless, in the full glare of the floodlights illuminating the spire, except for occasional neck and head movements. In the morning, preening and stretching began approximately one hour after sunrise, this activity culminating in two or three brief circuits around the spire before the birds departed south-eastwards to Chichester gravel pits. All the birds involved were immatures. Cormorants were again seen on the spire on a few occasions in late August and early September 1974 but failed to re-appear in 1975.

R. S. R. Fitter (1949, *London's Birds*, page 57) mentions single birds sitting on top of the steeple of a church at Ludgate Hill in July 1973 and on the summit of St Paul's Cathedral in August 1931. Two birds also frequented the top of Big Ben in June 1928. The *Handbook* also records the occasional use of other elevated positions such as chimneys. It would seem, however, that the numbers involved at Chichester, and the persistence of the habit for more than twelve weeks, are particularly unusual.

I am indebted to Mrs M. Marsden for drawing my attention to this behaviour and to Mrs J. Crawshaw for assistance in maintaining regular observations in 1973. **S. W. M. Hughes**

6 West Way, Slinford, Horsham, West Sussex RH13 7SB

More down-to-earth, and obviously loath to miss any opportunity is this Blue Tit:

Wakefulness of Blue Tit roosting in street lamp.—At 7 p.m. on 2nd January 1965, a fine and very dark night with the temperature below zero, I was walking near my house at Virginia Water, Surrey, when a shadow appeared on the road in the area of light thrown out by a street lamp. I expected to see an owl, but on looking up was surprised to find a small bird hopping about in some brambles underneath the lamp. I stood still and it flew straight to the lamp and without hesitation disappeared between the bulb and the glass shade. I walked over to the lamp and, looking up at the light, saw a Blue Tit *Parus caeruleus* sitting on the upper edge of the glass shade under the metal reflector. It immediately flew out again and went back to the brambles, but as soon as I left it returned to the lamp.

What surprised me most was that, even assuming it had previously been disturbed, the bird should have flown out of the shadows straight up to and past a brilliant light nearly three hours after dark.

Douglas Carr

[The roosting of Blue Tits in street lamps is well known in London (see *The Birds of the London Area since 1900*: 238) and is regular in Salisbury, Wiltshire, and other places (*Brit. Birds,* 54: 287-288), but in this case the activity long after dark seems unusual.—EDS.]

Roosting is a field where Wrens seem to have taken a leaf from the *Guinness Book of Records* – not in this case cramming students into a Mini or a 'phone box but:

Over 60 Wrens roosting together in one nest box Mr and Mrs T. J. Dove, my neighbours at High Kelling, Norfolk, have a nest box on the wall by the back door of their bungalow. The space inside it is 4½ inches wide, 5½ inches deep and 5¾ inches high, and it has a hole of two inches diameter. Just before dusk on 7th February 1969, at the start of a period of very cold weather, numbers of Wrens *Troglodytes troglodytes* were seen creeping along a holly hedge towards the box. After that Mr and Mrs Dove and I, accompanied once by Dr and Mrs N. W. Cusa, kept watch on several evenings from a workshop with a glass-topped door only a few feet away. Through the windows on two sides we could also see the Wrens gathering in the garden from all directions. They began to arrive from about 5.50 p.m., getting a little later each evening as the daylight lengthened, until 21st February when a thaw came and they dispersed. On one evening all seemed to have entered in 15 minutes and yet on another occasion late-comers were arriving after half an hour.

Sometimes it was impossible to get an accurate count as a few were still creeping in when it grew too dark to see. We counted 46, 49 and 60 Wrens entering the box on different nights and saw that the last arrivals had great difficulty in getting inside. So Mr Dove put up a second box close by and on the following night there was much flying in and out of both, though most of the Wrens settled in the original box. The highest minimal count was 61 in the main box (which meant only 2.33 cubic inches per bird) and seven in the overflow, besides three which were last seen outside. Sometimes the latest arrivals made about six individual attempts to enter before three or four together got in with an apparently concerted effort. Mrs Dove watched on several mornings and found that the Wrens took about 20 minutes to emerge. One or two would perch at the entrance, peering round for a while before flying off, and then another one or two would take their place. They came in and went out in silence. One Wren was found dead in the box.   WINIFRED U. FLOWER
Woods Corner, 18 Heathfield Road, High Kelling, Holt, Norfolk

The Reverend Edward A. Armstrong, author of the monograph on *The Wren* (1955), comments: 'These must surely be record numbers. The highest total known to me otherwise is 46 in one box (P. Leybourne, quoted in *The Handbook*, 1944 edition, 5: 293). There is also an instance of 31 in a box in America (C. E. Ehinger, 1925, *Murrelet*, 6: 37-39). When Wrens roost communally, individuals are occasionally found dead, but this is probably due to the effects of cramped quarters on already debilitated birds rather than to suffocation alone.' EDS

After that, who could express any surprise at these accounts of curious behaviour in several species?

WREN SWIMMING.

I HAVE recently observed some rather curious behaviour of a Wren (*Troglodytes t. troglodytes*).

About four yards from my garage door is a rain water tank full to the brim with water. On going to the garage on November 19th, 1946, I saw a Wren bathing in the water, and not on the iron rim of the tank. The bird flew off at my appearance. I went behind the garage door and looked out of a small hole to watch. Presently the Wren came back and perched on the iron rim of the tank. After a look round it took off and swam round in a semi-circle and landed back on the rim. It rode the water most buoy-antly, fluttering its wings a little as it swam. The water was quite two feet deep. The Wren seemed to enjoy the performance and it swam round the tank several times again, doing all the motions of a bird bathing when it reached the rim again.

One is apt to forget how buoyant all birds must be in water—for a time. FRED S. TRITTON.

Red-legged Partridges attracted by music In March 1976, while attempting to photograph Red-legged Partridges *Alectoris rufa* from a car at Grainthorpe, Lincolnshire, I found that these birds were affected to a remarkable extent by music from the car radio. Although a close

approach was frequently possible, most started to run away as soon as I switched off the car engine. When I then experimented by leaving the car radio on, so that the change in noise level was less noticeable, I was able to photograph several partridges feeding normally. To my surprise, however, some seemed attracted by the 'pop' records being played and, on two separate days, one particular individual approached closely and stood listening intently under the open car window for about ten minutes. Others sang in accompaniment to the records, with a subdued, twittering warble. The rarer Partridges *Perdix perdix* were less approachable and seemed completely unaffected by the music.   KEITH ATKIN
5 Hazel Grove, Louth, Lincolnshire LN11 8RU

TREE-CREEPER CLIMBING A MAN.

THE following incident, I think, well exemplifies the overwhelming and inborn instinct in the Tree-Creeper (*Certhia familiaris britannica*) to climb up anything rather than remain on the ground.

On May 30th, 1944, half an hour after a brood had left their nest in my garden, I was watching one of the fledglings clinging to the trunk of a tree when it spotted a parent and attempted to fly to it. But it missed its mark and fell on the ground about six feet from an old pine.

I at once walked up to it to get a close-up view, but as soon as I stood perfectly still it leapt on to a turn-up of my trousers and, with ease and vigour, climbed my clothes until it reached my shoulder, all the time uttering shrill squeaks.   Apparently seeing that it could go no higher, it fluttered to the base of the pine and forthwith climbed up it until it reached a low, dead branch along which it crept upside down almost to the tip—a distance of ten feet.   From there it flew to a nearby tree on which it very quickly climbed to a height of over twenty feet.

I wonder if any other field observer can claim the distinction and privilege of having been climbed by a Tree-Creeper !   B. H. RYVES.

House Sparrows dust-bathing in sugar.—During the winter of 1962-63, but well before the onset of the cold weather, House Sparrows (*Passer domesticus*) began to dust-bathe in sugar bowls on the tables in our works canteen in Derby, which they enter through the ventilators.   The habit developed—sometimes they seemed almost to be 'queuing up' for a bathe—and continues even now, months afterwards, if the canteen staff fail to cover the bowls.   The sparrows bathe in exactly the same manner as in heaps of sand in the factory yard.   The sugar is the ordinary granulated white variety; it remains very dry in the warm canteen and does not seem to stick to their feathers.   Finally, it should be added that ants have never been seen in the canteen and so there can be no question that the birds are anting or that they were originally attracted to the sugar by these insects.

C. GOODWIN

Carrion Crows hanging upside down from electricity cables
In the Staplehurst area of Kent, on 26th December 1973, I was
surprised to see a Carrion Crow *Corvus corone* hanging upside down
from an electricity cable. Two others were also perched on the wires
and several more were feeding on the ground. Three days later,
8 km east of Staplehurst, I saw another Carrion Crow hanging
upside down from an electricity wire. Again there were others both
on the wires and on the ground. In this latter instance the bird
righted itself, thus completing a somersault. I suggest that these
birds were 'playing' and derived 'pleasure' from their experience
rather in the way that Ravens *C. corax* appear to enjoy aerobatic
tumbling. The only references I can find relating to such
behaviour among the Corvidae are of a Carrion Crow perching
upside down (*Brit. Birds*, 46: 378, which also refers to *Brit. Birds*,
42: 327); a Rook *Corvus frugilegus* somersaulting on a wire (*Brit.
Birds*, 54: 121-122); and a Rook and a Hooded Crow *C. c. cornix*
hanging upside down from wires (*Brit. Birds*, 57: 182-183).

D. ELPHICK

28 Coniston Drive, Holmes Chapel, Crew, Cheshire

Rook somersaulting on wire.—On 1st November 1960, near Colchester, Essex, I saw a Rook (*Corvus frugilegus*) hanging upside down by its feet from high tension wires about eighty feet up. It appeared to be dead. Two or three other Rooks were perched on the same wire. I turned away and, on looking back a minute or two later, I was astonished to see that the "dead" bird had vanished. Then, as I watched, a Rook slowly and deliberately leant forward and turned a somersault round the wire, holding on to it all the time with its feet and flapping its wings about twice to pull itself upright again. It repeated this somersault slowly several times, pausing for a few seconds between each circle. Finally it went forward again and hung vertically downwards with its wings closed. It stayed in this position for two or three seconds, then dropped from the wire and flew back to it, after which it flew away.

The whole action was very amusing to watch and I had the impression that the bird was "playing". The wire was separated from adjacent ones by at least three feet, probably more, and the Rook could not possibly have made electrical contact. It was not stunned or injured in any way, but appeared perfectly well and in the intervals between somersaulting sat composedly. It flew quite normally.

R. V. A. MARSHALL

The unbiased observer might be just as puzzled if watching these goings-on from a distance:

Calling up a Corncrake.—Some friends and I were motoring near Ballinluig, Perthshire, on 22nd May 1954, when we heard a Corncrake (*Crex crex*) calling from a patch of nettles where a small stream flowed under the road. Despite the fact that it was only 5 a.m. we were sufficiently enthusiastic to pull up a little way past the area and retrace our steps. As might be expected, the bird stopped calling as we drew near and our efforts to flush it were in vain; it did not start to call again until we had almost returned to the car. On hurrying back to the territory with great caution, we were grateful to see the bird as it stood—head well up—calling in the low weed growth. One of us produced a comb in an endeavour to attract the bird in the way suggested in many books—the effect was nil. Time seemed ripe for one of my bird imitations and so I contrived to produce a series of notes that sounded, more or less, like a Corncrake. The effect was—to say the least—electrical: the bird ceased calling and hastily made towards me, only stopping when it reached the wall alongside the bridge. I moved to the end of this wall and lay down behind the roadside herbage calling all the while. The bird quickly arrived at a position about one foot from my head.

After this it seemed possible to catch the bird so I crossed the road, stood beside the stream and started to "crake". The Corncrake ran under the bridge and approached me—there was no cover of any sort and it had every opportunity of seeing that my friends and I were not Corncrakes. The bird was not deterred, however, and came to my feet. When I stopped calling it ran off a little distance, but after I had squatted and was holding my hand in readiness to catch the bird, it returned the instant I started calling. On seeing my hand it grasped my little finger in its bill in a most aggressive manner—I felt rather harshly treated and hoped that this was not customary Corncrake courting. This development enabled me to grasp the bird and within ten minutes we had absorbed the plumage details, ringed it and returned it to the nettle patch.

The event seems to indicate (or confirm) that the prime means of locating a mate or a rival is by sound, for even my "uncorncrake-like" bulk did not lessen the bird's interest in me and my onlooking friends were completely disregarded. We subsequently motored to Skye and heard other Corncrakes calling—I tried the mimicry again twice but without any success.   J. W. DONOVAN

Birds are undoubtedly adaptable – not to mention ingenious – usually with good purpose.

Incubating Moorhen repeatedly pulling cover over itself in rain
During an all-night fishing session at a disused clay pit near Snaith, Yorkshire, on 24th-25th May 1969, A. Smith, C. Bowyer and I saw a brooding Moorhen *Gallinula chloropus* behaving in an unfamiliar way. Just after we had taken up our pitches on the bank in the early evening, I noticed the Moorhen on its nest a few yards out from the bank and about 15 yards away to my right at the edge of a bed of short and sparse *Phragmites*. A.S. was much farther to my right, and C.B. on my left, neither being able to see the bird from their pitches. About one foot from the nest I noticed a very dirty piece of polythene about a foot square. At about 20.00 BST it began to rain heavily and, after some two minutes, the Moorhen stood up on its nest, moved one leg, reached forward and downward and picked up the polythene with its bill. It then arranged this over its back, pushing it into place with shuffling movements of its bill. The whole operation, taking only about a minute, was performed very skilfully and deliberately, and appeared to be customary behaviour in such circumstances. Its movements were reminiscent of a bird manipulating nest material while brooding. The polythene had the appearance of a cape, covering the entire back and sides, with only the head and neck protruding at the front. I immediately called my colleagues over and they came and looked at it with the 'cape' in position.

The heavy rain lasted for most of the night, and I erected waterproof sidescreens which prevented me from seeing the nest. A.S. came over three times in the rain and noted that, whenever he passed, the Moorhen hurriedly left the nest, dislodging the polythene; almost

at once it returned and resumed brooding, covering itself as before. He watched this behaviour for two or three minutes on each occasion. By dawn the rain had stopped and I noticed that the polythene was once more beside the nest. A further short shower started at about 05.00 BST, however, and some two minutes later the Moorhen again covered itself with the plastic sheet. By this time I had stopped fishing and was able to direct my full attention to the bird. The rain stopped, and about ten minutes later the Moorhen turned its head round, and, grasping the edge of the piece of polythene in its bill, flicked it sideways to land beside the nest about a foot away as before.

The polythene was the only piece of flotsam in the vicinity and the Moorhen was apparently using it deliberately to shelter itself and the nest from the rain, removing it just as purposely after the rain had stopped.　　　　　　　　　　　　　　　　　A. F. HAWKINS
Department of Botany, The University, Leeds 2

HOUSE-SPARROW PLUCKING FEATHERS FROM WOOD-PIGEON.

ON April 21st, 1947, I was watching a pair of Wood-Pigeons (*Columba p. palumbus*) in Bloomsbury Square, London. A female House-Sparrow (*Passer d. domesticus*) flew up, perched on a branch about three feet away from the two birds and then attacked the under tail-coverts of one of the birds, removing a feather. It flew off (probably to its nesting site) returning in ten to fifteen seconds; the Wood-Pigeon made a few half-hearted pecks, but again it was successful in obtaining a feather or feathers. This was repeated four times, the House-Sparrow once taking such a peck that seven feathers floated down.　　　　　　　　　　GWYNETH M. HARRISON.

It is difficult to assess whether the House Sparrow was being especially cheeky, or if the Woodpigeons were just rather thick!

Feathers, we all know, are used in many birds' nests – but have we paused to think of the labour involved?

NUMBER OF FEATHERS IN NESTS OF LONG-TAILED TIT.

DURING the nesting season of 1922 I obtained two perfectly normal nests of the Long-tailed Tit (*Ægithalos caudatus roseus*) with the object of ascertaining the number of feathers in each. A very careful count was made, with the result that 802 were found in the first nest and 1,518 in the second. It is surprising to see such a wide difference in the totals and to know that the lining of a single nest contained more than 1,500 feathers. D. W. MUSSELWHITE.

[Macgillivray, *Brit. Birds*, II., p. 458, gives 2,379 as the contents of one nest, and Mr. R. H. Read records, *Bull. B.O.C.*, XIX., p. 22, 952 feathers in a nest examined by him.—EDS.]

NUMBERS OF FEATHERS IN NESTS OF LONG-TAILED TIT.

WITH reference to the note on this subject (*antea*, p. 189), the following record may be of interest. A nest of the Long-tailed Tit was found at Aldworth, Berkshire, on June 17th, 1922, and appeared to be of normal size. On counting the feathers, it was found that the total was 2,457. A. STEVEN CORBET.

WITH reference to Mr. D. W. Musselwhite's note (*antea* p. 189) on the difference in the numbers of feathers in two nests of the Long-tailed Tit (*Ægithalos caudatus roseus*) examined by him, the following particulars of six nests examined by me seem to show that the number of feathers in the nest is largely a question of the distance of the nest from a farmyard or poultry run where feathers can be obtained.

Number of feathers.		Distance from nearest farmyard.
No. 1	2024	120 yards
No. 2	1660	325 ,,
No. 3	1573	400 ,,
No. 4	1203	450 ,,
No. 5	971	560 ,,
No. 6	835	650 ,,

The distances were carefully measured on a six-inch ordinance survey. E. U. SAVAGE.

NUMBER OF FEATHERS IN NESTS OF LONG-TAILED TIT.

WITH reference to the note by the Rev. E. U. Savage (*antea*, p. 217), on the number of feathers in six nests of the Long-tailed Tit (*Ægithalos caudatus roseus*) and the distance of each nest from the nearest source of supply. A further analysis of the figures given leads to a most interesting result. On the assumption that only one feather was brought on each trip the total mileage travelled by these six pairs of birds in obtaining feathers works out as follows :—

Nest No. 1	..	..	..	276 miles.
,, No. 2	..	..	..	612 ,,
,, No. 3	..	..	..	716 ,,
,, No. 4	..	..	..	616 ,,
,, No. 5	..	..	..	618 ,,
,, No. 6	..	..	..	618 ,,

The remarkable similarity in most of these distances is, to say the least, surprising, and it would almost seem to suggest that the birds have only a certain amount of energy to expend on each process of nest-building, and that when that amount of energy has been used the process will cease, regardless of the number of feathers obtained. In the case of Nest No. 1 it is possible that an ample supply of feathers was obtainable before the energy allowance had been exhausted, but the similarity in distance in the other five cases would certainly seem to call for some explanation. Further investigation into the question would be of interest.

A. ASTLEY.

'Unusual nesting sites', listed in human terms, are legion, but few are as unusual as these:

UNUSUAL NESTING SITE OF WREN.

ON July 7th, 1946, I was shown the nest of a Wren (*Troglodytes t. troglodytes*) built on a ledge beneath a portable iron saw bench about four feet square, in which was a small circular saw. The saw was in continuous use daily from about 9.0 a.m. to 5.0 p.m., and was belt-driven by a noisy motor engine a few feet away. The teeth of the saw were about six to eight inches from the nest. The nest was built and some eggs laid when the bench was moved to another spot in the wood, 40 yards away : one egg fell out on to some sawdust, but was replaced. The birds followed the bench and reared their young, which were 7-8 days old when I saw the nest. They fledged safely a few days later.

H. R. TUTT.

THRUSH INCUBATING IN TRAIN IN MOTION.

THE following interesting note appeared in the *Belfast News-letter* for May 8th, 1914 :—

An interesting incident in bird-life has recently been noted at Limavady. A Thrush was observed frequently in the vicinity of a number of carriages lying on a siding at the railway station. It was apparently engaged in nesting operations, and although the carriages ran out daily (Sundays excepted) twice to Limavady Junction and once to Londonderry, returning each evening at 4.50, later observation elicited the fact that a nest had been built underneath a first-class composite carriage, immediately over the steam-heating pipe, and contained four eggs. Notwithstanding the regular journeys the parent bird continued to care for the eggs, and much kindly interest was manifested in its doings by the railway officials, both at Londonderry and Limavady. The alteration in the train service, which came into force on the 1st May, led the mother-Thrush to experience the annoyance of " missing the train," for on her return to Londonderry Waterside Station on the evening of the 1st inst., after a foraging expedition, she found, doubtless to her intense dismay, that the train had disappeared, having left for Limavady at 4.40 instead of 4.50 under the revised time-table. The bird's predicament was observed at Londonderry, and Mr. J. Candy, station-master, telephoning to Mr. W. Conly, station-master at Limavady, reported the mishap, and jocularly observed that the Thrush would probably journey to Limavady on the axle of the next train, and to look out for it. It is not known how the bird travelled, but at a later hour the same evening it was seen at Limavady, resuming its labours on the nest. Pending the hatching of the eggs the carriage has been withdrawn from use by the sympathetic officials.

On reading the above extraordinary story, I wrote to the station-master at Limavady for confirmation and for further particulars, and I give his reply to me.

Midland Railway Co.—Northern Counties Committee,
Limavady Station, 16.5.1914.

DEAR SIR,—This is a true story. The set of carriages under one of which the nest has been built, makes three trips daily, Sundays excepted, here to Limavady Junction at 8.10 a.m. and right back to here ; here to Limavady Junction at 10.20 a.m. and right back to here ; here to Derry at 11.35 a.m. and return from Derry at 4.40 p.m.

The nest was only discovered on May 5th. When the man at Derry who examines all carriages was carrying out his duties the bird flew off, but resumed on the nest before the return of the train in the evening.

On the 6th inst. she again left the nest on arrival in Derry to procure food, etc., but unfortunately she missed the train that evening. The train formerly left Derry at 4.50 p.m., and I presume the change had something to do with her missing the train. However, she was here again the following morning. It got into the Press, and so many people were examining the nest and actually putting their hands into it to prove the question of eggs, that she left it for ever. . . . To prevent trespassers on the line I had to remove the nest to the office here, and of course the eggs are now lost.

Now this carriage travelled regularly (Sundays excepted) about fifty miles daily, while the nest was being built and until she forsook it, about the 9th inst.

I have many enquiries from different parts of the country, as it is really a rare occurrence.

I am, yours respectfully,
WILLIAM CONLY, *Station-master.*

I am sure very few, if any, of your readers had any idea that a bird would sit on a jolting train, and it is only a pity she was not allowed to hatch out her eggs.   W. H. WORKMAN.

[There are some discrepancies between the account in the *Belfast Newsletter* and that furnished by Mr. Conly, but we presume the latter may be taken as correct.   Instances of nests built on trucks and carriages in sidings are not uncommon, but it is certainly extraordinary to find a bird continuing to sit for so long under such conditions.—EDS.]

ROBIN NESTING ON A BED IN AN OCCUPIED ROOM.

ON April 28th, 1929, in response to a letter from Mr. M. P. Pollack, of Kendal End, Barnt Green, near Birmingham, I went to see the nest of a Robin (*Erithacus r. melophilus*) built on a bed in his house.   The bird was sitting on the nest when I saw it, and it was about four feet from the open window. Mr. Pollack has since kindly furnished me with full particulars of the occurrence.

At the end of March, one morning, he noticed some leaves on the dressing-table ; they appeared to have been blown in at the window, so they were swept away.   Next day, more leaves were found on the end of the bed, in the " tunnel " caused when the bed-clothes were thrown over the end of the bed in the early morning.   These were also cleared away, but in a day or two a Robin was seen bringing them, and accordingly a cardboard box was supplied, and the nest was built in this.

The nest was begun on April 1st and completed on the 13th or 14th.   The first egg was laid on April 16th, about 6.45 a.m., the second on the 17th about 6.30, the third on the 18th about 7.30, the fourth on the 19th about 7, the fifth on the 20th about 7.30.   The hen did not sit regularly till April 27th. The eggs were hatched on May 6th about 6 a.m.   Both parents continually fed the young.   The young left the nest at about 5 a.m. on May 19th.   During the day the young flew about the room, and then found their way out, with one or other of the parents.

I understand that the bed was in regular use ; of course the window was kept open all the time.   H. G. ALEXANDER.

Birds as food for other animals have not so far featured in this book, but surely few dainty morsels could be as tempting as a Goldcrest.

Goldcrests killed by edible frogs On the Danish island of Christiansø, in the Baltic Sea, the edible frog *Rana esculenta* is a common resident, and the Goldcrest *Regulus regulus* a very numerous spring and autumn migrant. Goldcrests often feed on the muddy shores and among branches in the shallow water of one of the small ponds; they are often very tame and can be watched closely by members of the bird observatory. On 21st September 1976, we observed a Goldcrest 'swimming', with a medium-sized frog anchored to its tail. The Goldcrest protested a little, but otherwise it just appeared to be wondering what was happening. At this moment, a large frog swam vigorously towards the two; when about 10 cm ahead of the Goldcrest, it pushed forward and grasped the bird from the front; with a splash, the frog dived with its victim, both remaining submerged for several minutes. Two days later, we observed a similar incident, in which a Goldcrest was grasped very proficiently by its head and breast; before it went under, we had the pathetic last sight of a little tail between two legs, one of them bearing one of our observatory rings. On a third occasion, we observed a medium-sized frog 'playing' with a Goldcrest, which eventually drowned, while on a nearby shore two large frogs were resting with a drowned Goldcrest between them. The impression of the frogs as miniature crocodiles was striking. It was not established whether the frogs swallowed the birds, but the big ones would certainly be able to do so. Although we have no observations of frogs preying on other bird species, we once saw them following a Siberian Chiffchaff *Phylloscopus collybita tristis* with great interest.

JØRGEN RABØL
Universitetets Zoologiske Laboratorium, Universitetsparken 15,
DK-2100 Copenhagen, Denmark

Marsh frogs seizing birds On the afternoon of 20th August 1974, in the Ebro Delta, Tarragona, Spain, following a morning of continuous heavy rain and increasing wind, we watched a grounded Bonelli's Warbler *Phylloscopus bonelli* feeding on low herbage beside a track separating rice-paddy from a reed-fringed lake. Shortly afterwards we heard a distress call and saw a medium-sized marsh frog *Rana ridibunda* dragging the warbler by the wing across the track towards the lake. We rescued the warbler unharmed and ringed it: a first-year with no visible subcutaneous fat and the unusually low weight of 5.6 g (23 Bonelli's Warblers mist-netted in Spain averaged 8.18 g, range 6.2–10.1 g). On 19th September 1977, at Lake Koronia, Macedonia, Greece, a Yellow Wagtail *Motacilla flava* mist-netted at a roost over mud and water on the shore was hanging below the net caught only by one wing, about 8 cm clear of the surface, when its free wing was seized by a 6-cm long marsh frog. The frog was not heavy enough to pull the wagtail down and released it when closely approached. The first incident is similar to those described by J. Rabøl (*Brit. Birds* 71: 85) in which Goldcrests *Regulus regulus* were killed by edible frogs *Rana esculenta* in the baltic, and suggests that exhausted birds may be especially vulnerable. Hellmich (1962, *Reptiles and Amphibians of Europe*, p. 74) stated that small birds are among the favourite prey of marsh frogs.

P. J. Belman and P. A. I. Eddings
107 Grange Road, Ealing, London W5 3 PH

Acute readers will have noted here, and in the case of the Corncrake mentioned earlier, a distinct alertness and adaptability on the part of bird ringers!

Sometimes, bird 'food' is inexplicable: a very risky substitute for grit? Or not, apparently, very filling:

Starling eating glass fragments On 22nd May 1971, at Lawrence Weston, Bristol, I saw an adult Starling *Sturnus vulgaris* probing in a small heap of broken glass beside a main road. It picked up and swallowed a spicule ½–1 cm in length and then a second of about the same size before flying off. On inspecting the heap of glass I could find no evidence of organic material which might have attracted the bird in the first place. I thought the glass had been swallowed as a substitute for grit, although there seemed to be no shortage of that in the area. It appears that the question is more complex, however: according to Colonel R. Meinertzhagen, in *A New Dictionary of Birds* (1964: 341), Starlings use small shells instead of grit to aid the digestion of vegetable matter; also, it seems likely that in spring the Starling would have been eating mainly animal food.   A. P. Radford

2 Wyck Beck Road, Brentry, Bristol BS10 7JE

Herring Gull attempting to catch snowflakes In mid January 1977, during a light fall of snow at Falmouth, Cornwall, I saw four Herring Gulls *Larus argentatus* on a ridge roof outside my office. One, an adult, was walking about, lunging in this direction and that, trying to catch the larger of the snowflakes in its beak. When the snow stopped, it preened a little and flew off.   T. J. S. PINFIELD
2 Well Lane, Constantine, Falmouth, Cornwall

Sometimes, too, birds get into the same sort of tangle as a child with a toffee apple, or an adult with a crumbling cream cake!

Woodpigeon trapped by slice of bread.—On 25th May 1964, on Wandsworth Common, London, I saw a Woodpigeon *Columba palumbus* standing motionless on the ground with a slice of white bread completely encircling its neck.   The bread was not in the least old or dirty and the Woodpigeon had presumably put its head through it while, as is customary with birds, eating the centre first.   When I approached to within 20 yards it flew away low and settled again motionless about 150 yards away, the bread still firmly in place. ·
                                   JOHN GOODERS

As the parent of young, inexhaustible and apparently unfillable children (and living in a house with several nestfuls of noisy Starling youngsters under the eaves) it is easy for me to sympathise with this parent Blackbird:

Blackbird thrusting nesting-material into fledgling's mouth.—During the latter half of April, 1953, in my garden at Churchdown, Gloucester, a very tame female Blackbird (*Turdus merula*), who had successfully reared a first brood a few days earlier in one of my honeysuckles, appeared two or three yards from me and I was interested to see that she had her beak full of dried grasses, evident sign that she was building a second nest. At this moment one of the first brood rushed up to her with the usual flapping wings and loud squawkings to indicate desire to be fed. I watched with much interest to see in what way the mother bird would respond to two clashing instincts. She instantly dropped the grass, and appeared to pick up some small morsel, and thrust it into the open beak of the young bird. As she had made no search for food I suspected it was something very small, or even that it was nothing at all, and was only a kind of token satisfaction of the instinct to put something into the gaping beak. The squawking went on as before. The mother-bird repeated her action two or three times, then as if she could stand the noise and flutterings no longer she picked up her bundle of grass and thrust the whole lot into the throat of the unfortunate young bird. It was amusing to see the latter ejecting it and I wished I could know what its mental reactions to its mother at that moment were. From the mother's point of view the remedy was quite effective in stopping the nuisance for the time at any rate.   A. A. G. WHITEHOUSE.

The sheer diversity of feeding behaviour shown by the Turnstone must establish some sort of record:

Turnstones searching for food in roof gutters.—During the first two weeks of September 1962 I paid several visits to Newlyn, Cornwall, where I noticed that the sloping roof of a long warehouse used for sorting fish was a roosting place for many dozens of gulls of various species. The droppings of these birds had whitened much of the roof and had apparently helped to silt up portions of the surrounding gutters. In these gutters three or four Turnstones *Arenaria interpres* were often to be seen actively searching for food by probing into the silt or occasionally flicking pieces to one side. Less frequently they also poked about in the crevices of the roof. Every now and then one would find and swallow something edible, but, except for a few small worms, most of the prey could not be identified. Although I had visited the Newlyn district at the same season for the previous sixteen years, this was the first time that I had noticed such behaviour by Turnstones.   BERNARD KING

Turnstone feeding on dead sheep.—On 1st March 1964, a day of heavy mist, we were walking along the shore at Steart Point, Somerset, when we came across the carcase of a sheep. A Carrion Crow *Corvus corone* and two Great Black-backed Gulls *Larus marinus* flew from it and settled a short distance away. Part of the sheep's abdomen had been eaten away and on closer inspection we were surprised to see the tail of a Turnstone *Arenaria interpres* protruding from the partially exposed rib cage. The rhythmic movements of this tail suggested that its owner was feeding inside the thoracic cavity. As we circled round in an attempt to get a better view of what was happening, however, it backed out and, hopping on to the rib cage, paused there momentarily before flying to join a large flock of Turnstones on the shore.

The movements of the Turnstone's tail had certainly indicated a feeding action and, although we did not actually see it with flesh in its bill, we felt safe in assuming that it had been eating the viscera. The corpse was very fresh, still with uncongealed blood in the thoracic cavity, and we saw no crustaceans, insects or parasites on which the Turnstone might alternatively have been feeding.

Colin Selway and Michael Kendall

Turnstones feeding on human corpse.—On 2nd February 1966, whilst walking along a beach in south-west Anglesey, I saw five Turnstones *Arenaria interpres* and a Carrion Crow *Corvus corone* feeding on what I at first took to be a pig washed up by the tide and partly covered by wind-blown sand. When I reached the object, however, I discovered that it was a human corpse which had been in the water for some considerable length of time. The birds had been feeding on the facial muscles and the neck. I should perhaps add that I actually saw the Turnstones tearing off small shreds of flesh after the Carrion Crow had removed some bigger pieces; there was therefore no doubt that they were feeding on the corpse itself and not on sandhoppers or other invertebrates attracted to this food source. A. J. Mercer

[In recent years we have published records of Turnstones feeding on animal remains, ranging from the carcases of birds and a Wolf *Canis lupus* in arctic Canada (*Brit. Birds*, 55: 241-243) to those of a sheep and a probable cat in Britain (*Brit. Birds*, 58: 438; 59: 39). The above rather gruesome account seems to be the ultimate in necrophagous behaviour, however, and we think that it is now sufficiently established that Turnstones will probably turn to any animal carrion when the opportunity occurs.—Eds.]

As the editors comment: the gruesome ultimate! Although this is a striking demonstration of adaptability in a bird with a specialised feeding mechanism (the flattened beak to 'turn' over 'stones' like a shovel to dig out the small animals beneath), it is perhaps most appropriate to close with a demonstration of the ability to capitalise on man and his works that characterises today's most successful birds.

Magpies stealing boxed eggs   During May 1975, 'Live Letters', the correspondence section of the *Daily Mirror*, contacted me about a report they had received from Banstead, Surrey, of a Magpie *Pica pica* which attacked a papier maché carton of eggs left by the milkman and prised one out of the carton before being disturbed by a neighbour. The box had been closed and no egg would have been visible to the bird. After the publication of this report, another *Daily Mirror* reader, Mrs June Parramore, wrote about similar depredations by her local Magpies, at Ecclesfield, South Yorkshire. There, the milkman's customers leave bowls to be placed over the egg-cartons to protect them from Magpies, but the birds sometimes overturn these. Eggs have been attacked even in the storeroom, where they are kept in cartons inside a wooden box; the Magpies entered through a broken window and reached the eggs through the gaps in the wooden box. Since these incidents happened so far apart, it seems possible that this behaviour may already be quite widespread.

C. J. Mead

British Trust for Ornithology, Beech Grove, Tring, Hertfordshire HP23 5NR

⤚ 5 ⤙

Migration

Although, in Britain, the regular use of individually numbered metal bands or rings more or less coincided with the first publication of *British Birds*, it seems sensible to 'set the scene' for this tool in the study of birds – and particularly their migrations – with an historical review published some twenty years later.

EARLY BIRD-MARKING RECORDS.

To the Editors of BRITISH BIRDS.

SIRS,—This extract from Bewick's *British Birds* is interesting as being possibly the earliest record of bird-marking :—

"In 1797, a gamekeeper of E. M. Pleydell, Esq., of Whatcombe, Dorset, brought him a Woodcock, alive. Mr. P. put a thin brass ring with date on its leg.

"Following winter Mr. P. shot this bird in the same wood." Footnote, p. 63, Vol. II. (1805).

H. J. MOON.

[In point of date this Woodcock is beaten by a Swan, shot on Foulness Island, Essex, in Feb. 1776, and marked with a gold medal fastened to its neck, with the inscription "Le Roi Dame." The inscription is supposed to indicate that the bird was marked in Denmark. The record was published in *The Essex Chronicle* for 1776, and we are indebted to Mr. Miller Christy for drawing our attention to it.—EDS.]

EARLY BIRD-MARKING RECORDS.

To the Editors of BRITISH BIRDS.

SIRS,—On page 158 of this volume, Dr. H. J. Moon quotes from Bewick the case of a Woodcock marked in Dorset in 1797 and afterwards recovered at the same place. In an editorial note is added a record, from *The Essex Chronicle* of 1776, of a Swan bearing a medal indicating Danish origin. It may therefore be of interest to quote other old records, some of them of still earlier date. Doubtless the information which I can give by no means exhausts the subject.

Although Noah is recorded as having made homing experiments with a Dove, and less successfully with a Raven (*Genesis*, viii, 7–12), the earliest case of actual marking which I can cite is that given by Pliny in the tenth book of his *Natural History*. A Roman knight used to take some Swallows with him from Volaterrae in Tuscany to Rome, and to let them loose, for the information of his friends at home, after dyeing them with the colours of the winner of the chariot races.

The use of homing Pigeons is of great antiquity. There must also have been many early instances of marked captive birds, particularly those used in falconry, escaping and being recovered at a distance. One such is that of a Falcon belonging to Henry II., which escaped from Fontainebleau and was recovered at Malta, so it is said, twenty-four hours later. The story is given in various books, but I do not know its original source ; presumably it refers to the French king of the name (1519–59).

The case of the Swan in Essex is antedated by that of a Duck recorded by Gilbert White (letter to Daines Barrington, 12th February, 1771). This bird was shot in Sussex in the winter of 1708–9, and bore a silver collar engraved with the arms of the King of Denmark. One of White's editors, Harting, suggests that the bird may have been a Cormorant used in fishing. White himself adds " I have read a like anecdote of a Swan."

There is at least one case earlier than that quoted by Dr. Moon in which marking of wild birds was done in a spirit of more or less scientific inquiry. Lucanus (1922 : *Die Rätsel des Vögelzuges*) quotes a work by Johann Leonhard Frisch, published in 1740, in which the author records having tied coloured threads to the feet of Swallows. The birds returned next year, and as the dye was not washed out Frisch concluded that they had not hibernated under water !

Marking for purposes of migration study had been suggested even earlier than this. Schenk (1924: *Aquila*, 30–31, 325) and Quantz (1925 : *Ornithologische Monatsberichte*, 33, 14) quote a publication, dated 1722, in which it is recorded that one Gottlieb Koehlich, a pastor in east Prussia, had proposed marking White Storks, apparently old birds to be caught on the nest ; but this came to nothing.

It must have been very soon after the close of the eighteenth century that J. F. Naumann began the experiment, recorded in his work of 1822, to which attention has recently been drawn by the editor of the *Ornithologische Monatsberichte* (*loc. cit.*). Naumann released a number of Buzzards after marking them with copper rings upon which the complete data were inscribed. The account is in general terms only, but apparently a good many birds were marked over a period of years and a few were subsequently reported. The object was the study, not of migration, but of plumage changes, and for this no material was obtained.

In the nineteenth century, records of isolated marking experiments become fairly numerous. Lucanus mentions several German instances, referring especially to White Storks. Lühe (1908 : *Ornithologische Monatsberichte*, 16, 96) had already drawn attention to one interesting case, given by Homeyer (1881 : *Die Wanderungen der Vögel*), in which a Stork was marked in south-western Germany in July, 1880, and recovered in Spain a month later. This is in accord with recent experience.

Schenk (1921 : *Aquila*, 28, 152) mentions three early records of marked Storks which are supposed to have travelled from Europe to India, a movement not confirmed by twentieth century marking. In the two cases of which he is able to give details, the earlier dating from 1813, the birds are themselves alleged to have brought back with them the news of their winter capture.

Search would probably bring to light many early marking records in this country also. One, for instance, is quoted by Yarrell (1845 : *A History of British Birds*, 2nd ed., Vol. I., p. ix.) from the daily press of the year in which he wrote. It refers to a Swallow shot in Yorkshire which bore, tied to one leg, a piece of parchment inscribed " J. Rovina y Clavi. Barcelona, 10th March, 1845."

There is an antique, romantic flavour about this final record, quoted in various works from Slatin Pasha's *Fire and Sword in the Sudan* (1896). A young Crane liberated in south Russia by Falz-Fein, who has since used modern rings, was provided with a species of locket round its neck in which was placed a paper giving the bird's history in several languages. This was found soon afterwards near Dongola by a follower of the Mahdi, and was sent to Slatin, in his captivity at Omdurman, by the Khalifa. This, however, was in 1892, two years after Lord William Percy had begun the regular marking of Woodcock in Northumberland, and only seven years before Mortensen, in Denmark, inaugurated marking on a large scale with numbered rings.

A. LANDSBOROUGH THOMSON.

LONDON, 12th *November*, 1926.

We have to remember that, in the early years of this century, students of migration, when confronted with amazing feats on the part of birds (Eagle Clarke) or even with the more commonplace regular return to the same locality (Wilson), did not have the wealth of background information that is available to us today, and which has accrued from bird ringing.

THE FAR SOUTHERN WINTER QUARTERS OF THE ARCTIC TERN.

In working out the birds obtained by the Scottish National Antarctic Expedition, I found, to my great surprise, that all the Terns captured in widely scattered portions of the Weddell Sea, Antarctic Ocean, belonged to the most northern representative of their genus, namely, to *Sterna macrura*, the Arctic Tern !

Specimens were obtained between 64° 29′ and 72° 18′ S. latitude and from 12° 49′ to 35° 29′ W. longitude. They were often observed in considerable numbers, and are logged for March 5th, 1904, as being seen in thousands in 72° 31′ S. ; while from the 9th to the 13th of the same month, when off Coats Lands, in 74° 1′ S., 22° 0′ W., many were seen. Thus this bird so familiar to British Ornithologists would seem to have the most extensive latitudinal range to be found among vertebrate animals, since it is now known to occur from 82° N. to 74° 1′ S. It is at present the only Tern known to occur south of the Antarctic Circle.

The occurrence of this boreal species in the far-off ice fields of the South Polar Ocean during the northern winter season, is one of the most interesting zoological discoveries made by the many recent Antarctic expeditions. That it is only a winter visitor does not admit of doubt for the bird certainly does not breed there ; nor is any other Tern, so far as we know, a native of the Antarctic Continent. These very remarkable southern incursions are, no doubt, to be explained by the extraordinary abundance of food, especially of crustaceans swimming at or near the surface, to be found in the icy waters of the far south in the summer (our northern winter). This allures the Terns, and other birds, further and further towards the pole, until the great ice-barrier, which almost girdles the Antarctic Continent, arrests their further progress, since at its base the food supply entirely ceases.

WILLIAM EAGLE CLARKE.

MIGRATING BIRDS RETURNING TO THE SAME PLACE.

THERE have been many proofs that individual migrating birds return to the same place year after year, but as every well-proved instance of this habit is of value to the study of migration, it may be well to record the following :—

Among a large flock of Starlings which visits us every year in Cheshire there is a perfectly white bird. I have noticed this bird now for three successive years. It appears at the same time as the flock, and after careful inquiries I cannot find that it is ever seen after the flock has left. If ornithologists all around England would but trap birds and mark them, by a metal ring or otherwise, and advertise their having done so in this Magazine, how much we should be able to learn of their movements which we do not at present know. VICTOR WILSON.

[The plan of marking birds by an aluminium ring round the leg has often been tried, but never in a really systematic fashion. It would certainly teach us a great deal that cannot conceivably be learnt in any other way. To place rings on the legs of young birds just before they fledge would not be a great difficulty. We should like other readers' opinions on this matter.—EDS.]

The editorial footnote from volume one was a portentous one. Plans developed rapidly, both under the guidance of Harry Witherby, the editor of *British Birds*, and elsewhere.

MARKING BIRDS.

To the Editors of BRITISH BIRDS.

SIRS,—Some of the readers of BRITISH BIRDS may have seen in the " Field " of 11th January a note relating to the capture of a marked Teal in co. Kerry, Ireland. The bird had an aluminium plate round its leg with the name and address and a register number of the gentleman who marked it. As I have been for some time in communication with this gentleman (Herr Chr. Mortensen, of Viborg, Denmark) I thought a note of his work might be of interest.

Herr Mortensen for some years past has been catching various species of birds, and after marking them with an aluminium plate he has given them their liberty again, hoping in this way to trace the movements of these birds. Amongst the species thus marked were Starlings, Kites, White Storks, Goshawks, Common Buzzards, and Teal, and the results to date of these experiments were published in an interesting paper in the " Dansk Ornithologisk Forenings Tidsskrift," Part IV., 1907.

This Teal, I believe, was one of 100-200 marked during last autumn, and had been taken in the duck decoys there : it therefore had travelled about 850 miles W.S.W.

A Starling liberated on September 15th, 1904, was taken near Edinburgh, about 450 miles W.S.W., early in March, 1906. Should anyone come across any of Herr Mortensen's ringed birds at any time, it is hoped that they will send the ring, foot, and data of capture either to him direct or to me.

CLAUD B. TICEHURST.

Guy's Hospital, S.E.

[Mr. J. A. Harvie-Brown has also announced (*Ann. Scot. Nat. Hist.*, 1907, p. 114) that Mr. R. Tomlinson, of Musselburgh, had marked with a metal ring on the left foot a number of Starlings. Each ring was marked with a number, and the birds—115 in all—were liberated during December, 1906, and January and February, 1907.—EDS.]

A PLAN FOR MARKING BIRDS.

IN volume I. of this Magazine several communications were published on this subject. The advantage to students of migration of knowing exactly where birds travel by observations on marked birds is obvious ; but the difficulty of the plan is that so few birds which are marked are ever found again. If, however, great numbers were marked, no doubt a large enough percentage would turn up to make the results of value. Mr. C. Hawkins, of " Lyndhurst." Woodside Road,

South Norwood, informs us that he has had made a number of suitable aluminium rings of various sizes, stamped with a registered address (" Avis, Wye, Kent "), and each bearing a separate number for identification purposes. He is willing to supply these rings to anyone who will undertake to place them on birds, at the price of 5s. per gross, or 6d. per dozen. Mr. Hawkins also undertakes to keep a register of the particulars supplied by his correspondents concerning the birds marked, and to publish the results from time to time.

H. F. WITHERBY.

MARKED BIRDS.

ON the same lines as Herr Chr. Mortensen, of Viborg (*vide British Birds*, Vol. I., page 298), I have this year been marking and liberating a number of birds of various species. The mark employed is an aluminium ring on which is stamped " Ticehurst, Tenterden," and a register number, and the ring is put round one of the legs. Should any of my birds be met with by any readers of BRITISH BIRDS will they kindly return the ring and the leg to me, stating the locality and the date of capture ?

C. B. TICEHURST,
Hurstbourne, Tenterden, Kent.

MARKING BIRDS IN SCOTLAND.

MAY I trespass on your space to the extent of a few lines to draw the attention of readers of BRITISH BIRDS to a scheme for marking birds which we have just set afoot ? This inquiry into bird migration is to be carried out from the Natural History Department of the University of Aberdeen. The details are similar to those of the Rossitten enterprise, of which I have already given some description in these pages (Vol. II., p. 362). As I understand that our enterprise is to be closely followed by the appearance in the field of a similar one to be carried out under the auspices of this magazine, I cannot make any appeal here for co-operators to assist in the work of marking, and therefore confine myself to asking that any readers of BRITISH BIRDS finding one of our marked birds will return the ring, preferably with the foot or even the whole bird, with particulars of date, locality, etc., to " Bird Migration Inquiry, Natural History Department, The University, Aberdeen, N.B." We shall refund postage whenever desired. Our rings are marked " Aberdeen University " on the sizes for Lapwing and upwards, but we hope to get some returns for small birds marked with the contracted address (in smaller characters) " Abdn. Univ." There is a registered number on each ring.

A. LANDSBOROUGH THOMSON.

In Britain, the Witherby scheme rapidly became the major one, and these reports, written two and three years after its inception, indicate the enthusiasm and support generated.

MARKING BIRDS.

WE are very glad to be able to state that the scheme for marking birds with aluminium rings, outlined in our last number, has been well taken up, and we take this opportunity of thanking those of our readers who are helping by putting on the rings and filling up the schedules. We have so far issued nearly 3000 rings of various sizes, and we hope soon to publish some particulars of how they have been used, and meanwhile, as there will still be many young birds about during this month, we would ask those readers who have opportunities for joining in the work to apply for rings and schedules.

EDS.

MARKING BIRDS.

PROGRESS OF THE " BRITISH BIRDS' " SCHEME.

I AM glad to be able to report that so far as the number of birds marked is concerned, the results to date are extremely satisfactory. The demands for rings largely exceeded my expectations, and I regret that it was not always possible to supply them immediately in the quantities required. Between ten and eleven thousand rings have been sent out this year, and schedules recording the marking of between five and six thousand birds have already been returned.

When all the schedules have been sent in, I hope to give further details of the number of birds marked ; meanwhile I take the opportunity of sincerely thanking those who have spent so much time and labour in marking.

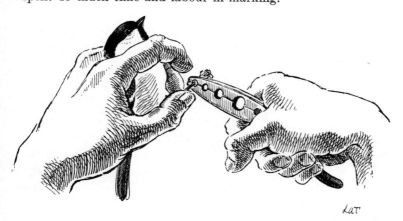

It is to be hoped that those into whose hands ringed birds fall will record their finds. It would greatly assist the enquiry if every reader of BRITISH BIRDS would advertise as widely as possible the fact that these birds have been ringed, and would point out that it is essential that we should be informed of (1) the number on the ring ; (2) the place where found, and (3) the date when found of *every* marked bird recovered.

H. F. WITHERBY.

It is, even now, easy to imagine the interest kindled by the first overseas recoveries trickling in to the Holborn office.

RECOVERY OF MARKED BIRDS.

COMMON TERN (*Sterna fluviatilis*).—B.B., No. 4308, marked by Messrs. Robinson and Smalley at Ravenglass, Cumberland, on July 30th, 1909, as a nestling. Recovered at Espiña, in Galicia, Spain, on September 21st, 1909.

This bird was caught by a boy, and was kept alive for two days. The capture was heard of by a coastguard named Inocente Dieguez, who reported the matter to the British Vice-Consul at Corcubion, who in turn reported it to Mr. Thomas Guyatt, the acting British Consul at Coruña. I am deeply indebted to Sir Edward Grey for drawing my attention to this case, and to Mr. Guyatt for very kindly undertaking the strictest enquiries with regard to the matter, and returning me the ring with full particulars of the capture of the bird.

This is particularly true when the migratory journey involved was a prodigious one. The first four Swallow recoveries from Africa are so noteworthy that each merits repetition – as does the jubilant note following the first.

A SWALLOW RINGED IN STAFFORDSHIRE AND RECOVERED IN NATAL.

THE following letter has just reached me :—

> Grand Hotel,
> Utrecht, Natal,
> *27th December*, 1912.

" Witherby,"
High Holborn, London.

DEAR SIR,

On December 23rd a Swallow was caught in the farmhouse of the farm " Roodeyand," 18 miles from this town, with a metal label round its leg, with the words : Witherby, High Holborn, London, and on the other side B.830.

The farmer, Mr. J. Mayer, took the label off and has it in his possession. As I am interested in birds of any sort and the migration of same, I shall be glad to know if you receive this letter safely.

Yours truly,

C. H. RUDDOCK, *Proprietor.*

The ring B.830 was put on an adult Swallow (*Chelidon r. rustica*) by Mr. J. R. B. Masefield, at Rosehill, Cheadle, Staffordshire, on May 6th, 1911. This bird was one of a pair (Mr. Masefield thought the female) which nested in a porch. Its mate was also caught and ringed. At the same time Mr. Masefield ringed another pair nesting in the same porch. In the summer of 1912 he again caught the Swallows which had come to nest in his porch and found that only one of them had a ring, viz. B.827, which was one of the birds nesting there the year before (see *supra*, p. 13). Neither its mate nor the other pair of which the present B.830 is one had returned to this particular spot.

That this Swallow breeding in the far west of Europe should have reached so far to the south-*east* of Africa as Natal, seems to me extraordinary. Unfortunately the few records we have as yet of ringed Swallows recovered during migration do not afford a clue to the routes taken and it seems to me unreasonable to suppose that our birds proceed southwards down the east side of Africa as *might* be inferred from this Natal record.

It is, indeed, quite impossible to theorize on a single recovery of this kind and we must be content at present with the bare fact—perhaps the most startling fact that the ringing of birds has as yet produced.

We are most thankful to Mr. Ruddock for reporting this extremely interesting recovery and we hope that the details of it will become widely known in South Africa and thus produce further results. H. F. WITHERBY.

THE SWALLOW RECOVERED IN NATAL.
To the Editors of British Birds.

Sirs,—If there was no other result of the Scheme for Ringing Birds organised by Mr. Witherby, the Swallow record from Natal is sufficient reward. May I, in this East African connection, draw attention to the Swift which was found dead in New Ross, co. Wexford, in May, 1886, with a piece of paper tied to it bearing the inscription " Mary Elsam, Suakin, Egypt, 10.3.86 " ? As I interviewed the man who found the bird and am satisfied the occurrence took place as above-stated, it may do no harm to mention this event, though already recorded in the *Birds of Ireland*, p. 103.   Richard M. Barrington.

[We have always regarded the record of the Swift with a piece of paper " tied under its tail " as having origin in a practical joke, perhaps perpetrated by a soldier recently returned from the Soudan. Is there any proof that the piece of paper was not tied on after the Swift's death ? What proof is there that it was tied on at Suakin ? As the Mahdi was in possession of the Soudan at the time and had advanced not far from Suakin, it may have been a clumsy attempt to make people suppose that one Mary Elsam was imprisoned there. But such " records," being of no scientific value whatever, should not be seriously considered.—Eds.]

SWALLOW RINGED IN AYRSHIRE AND RECOVERED IN THE ORANGE FREE STATE.

In August I received a letter from Mr. A. C. Theron dated from " Riet Vallei, District Lindley, O.F.S." stating that a Swallow had been captured bearing a ring with my name and address. As Mr. Theron gave neither the number of the ring nor the date of capture I asked him for these particulars and have just received his reply and the ring itself. The ring is number E937, and Mr. Theron informs me that the bird was captured at Riet Vallei on March 16th, 1913, and adds " I do not know when it arrived." This ring was placed on a nestling Swallow (*Chelidon r. rustica*) by Mr. R. O. Blyth at Skelmorlie, Ayrshire, on July 27th, 1912.

In our last volume (p. 277) an adult Swallow ringed in Staffordshire was recorded as having been captured near Utrecht, Natal, in December, and the present record is from about one hundred and fifty miles west of that place, which is not far in comparison with the total length of the journey.

In writing of the Natal record I expressed surprise that a Swallow breeding in the far west of Europe should migrate so far east in South Africa, but now that Dr. Hartert has shown (*Nov. Zool.*, Vol. XX.) by his observations in the middle of the Sahara that deserts are not necessarily a bar to the passage of migrating birds, as was formerly supposed, it may perhaps be presumed that these Swallows take a more direct line than one would previously have thought possible.

This second record, taken in conjunction with the first, is extremely valuable, and we are most grateful both to Mr. Blyth who ringed the Swallow and to Mr. Theron who reported it.

H. F. WITHERBY.

SWALLOW RINGED IN LANCASHIRE AND RECOVERED IN CAPE PROVINCE.

IT will interest readers of BRITISH BIRDS to learn that I have just received the following letter :—

SALEM,
NEAR GRAHAMSTOWN, C.P.,
SOUTH AFRICA.
February 6th, 1916.

To Witherby,
High Holborn, London.

SIR,

This morning I picked up here a dead Swallow and noticed a piece of metal bent around one leg just above the foot. This I took off and straightened out. On one side was a number 82620, on the other side was inscribed as near as I could make out, "Inform Witherby, High Holborn, London." I am therefore sending this in the hope that it will reach its destination, and prove of interest.

Yours faithfully,

S. GEO. AMM.

The bird referred to was a Swallow (*Chelidon r. rustica*), ringed as a nestling by Mr. F. W. Sherwood at Lytham, Lancashire, on July 3rd, 1915.

This is the third Swallow ringed under the BRITISH BIRDS Scheme which has been reported from South Africa. The first was ringed as an adult at Rosehill, Cheadle, Staffordshire, on May 6th, 1911, by Mr. J. R. B. Masefield, and was caught at a farm near Utrecht, Natal, on December 27th, 1912, and was kindly reported by Mr. C. H. Ruddock (Vol. VI., p. 277). The second was ringed as a nestling at Skelmorlie, Ayrshire, on July 27th, 1912, by Mr. R. O. Blyth, and was caught at Riet Vallei, Orange Free State, on March 16th, 1913, and kindly reported by Mr. A. C. Theron (Vol. VII., p. 167).

This third instance, two or three hundred miles further south and, like the others, in the eastern half of the continent, is extremely interesting, and makes it possible to state that, in any case, some of the Swallows which breed in various parts of the British Isles winter normally in the extreme south-east of Africa.

We tender our grateful thanks to Mr. Amm for informing us of this interesting event, and we must congratulate Mr. Sherwood on having ringed a bird which has been proved to have made so remarkable a journey.

H. F. WITHERBY.

SWALLOW RINGED IN YORKSHIRE FOUND IN SOUTH AFRICA.

I HAVE received the following letter from the Bishop of Glasgow :—

SIR,—I have just returned from South Africa. When in East Griqualand, staying with the Rev. M. Williamson of Ensikeni, Riverside Post, I was shown an aluminium ring that had been taken off a Swallow's leg. The bird was picked up about the 21st of February, 1919, in Michael Gwensa's cattle kraal. The ring was marked " Witherby, High Holborn, London," and inside were the letters and figures " J.M.53."

The Swallow was very thin and exhausted. The natives all thought it boded ill-luck for Michael, and considered that it was a clear case of witchcraft for a bird to appear from nowhere with a ring round its leg and alight in someone's cattle kraal !

ARCHIBALD GLASGOW & GALLOWAY.

This Swallow (*Hirundo r. rustica*) was ringed as a nestling by Mr. H. W. Robinson at Low Bentham, Yorkshire, on August 19th, 1918. I am sure that all the readers of *British Birds* will join me in thanking the Bishop of Glasgow for having transmitted this very interesting record.

This is the fourth Swallow ringed in Great Britain which has been found in South Africa, the others being : Staffordshire, adult, May 1911, Utrecht, Natal, December 1912 ; Ayrshire, nestling, July 1912, Orange Free State, March, 1913 ; Lancashire, nestling, July 1915, Grahamstown, Cape Province, February 1916. It is remarkable that all four have been found on the eastern side of South Africa. H.F.W.

Only in bird ringing are the frontiers of knowledge seen to be pushed back so spectacularly. An early Shelduck recovery heralded what we now know to be an annual migration to German estuaries in late summer, to pass the flightless period of moult in the safety of the enormous sand-flats.

SHELD-DUCK RINGED IN HAMPSHIRE RECOVERED IN GERMANY.

INCIDENTAL circumstances add to the interest of the following record of a Sheld-Duck (*Tadorna tadorna*), Case 906, ring " Aberdeen University 25886." This bird was marked as a duckling by Dr. Philip Gosse on July 16th, 1912, the locality

being Blackwater, Beaulieu, Hampshire. On August 18th, 1917, it was shot at Ost Eversand, at the mouth of the Weser, Germany. The information passed through several hands in the hope of finding an indirect means of communication, but it has in fact only recently reached me through Mr. Mortensen, the Danish bird-marker. This bird was one of a brood marked by Dr. Gosse and is the third member to be recorded. The other two recoveries have already been published (*Scot. Nat.*, 1915, p. 339), Case 447 having been reported from Saltash in February 1913, and Case 448 from Schleswig-Holstein in August 1913.　　　　　　A. LANDSBOROUGH THOMSON.

Before long, the Atlantic Ocean had been crossed by ringed birds, in both directions, in one twelve-month period.

PUFFIN RINGED AT ST. KILDA REPORTED IN NEWFOUNDLAND.

AN UNIQUE recovery of a ringed bird has just been reported to the Bird-ringing Committee, and is worthy of special mention outside the ordinary Recovery lists. A Puffin (*Fratercula a. grabæ*) was ringed (RV 4692) at St. Kilda by Lord Dumfries as a young one on August 10th, 1939, and was shot at Herring Neck, on the northern coast of Newfoundland on December 20th, 1939.　　　　　　ELSIE P. LEACH.

CASPIAN TERN RINGED IN U.S.A. FOUND IN YORKSHIRE.

IN *The Auk* for October, 1940 (p. 569), Mr. F. C. Lincoln, of the U.S. Biological Survey, makes the interesting announcement that a Caspian Tern (*Hydroprogne caspia*) ringed as a nestling, No. 566280, at the large colony on Shoe Island, in northern Lake Michigan on July 14th, 1927, was reported as found dead on the shore at Whitby, Yorks, in August, 1939. The band was sent to the Bureau of the Biological Survey and has been verified.

The Caspian Tern is a very rare vagrant to this country. Some thirty occurrences are on record and most of these have been on the east coast of England. This fact has seemed to point to Europe as their origin and probably most of them did come from the east, but the present record shows that it is possible for the bird to come from America and yet reach our east coast.

Mr. Lincoln, following the *A.O.U. Check-List*, calls the American bird *Hydroprogne caspia imperator*, but I have been unable to find any constant difference between American and Palæarctic birds. The same conclusion was reached by the late Dr. E. Hartert and more recently Dr. J. C. Peters in his *Check-List of the Birds of the World* (Vol. II, 1934, p. 331) has pronounced against the separation of the American bird as a recognizable race.　　　　　　H. F. WITHERBY.

Today, half a million or more birds are ringed in Britain each year, and findings of between ten and fifteen thousand marked birds are reported. Recoveries of British-ringed birds span the globe, coming from the east (150°E) of Russia – a Pochard; from 60°S of the equator in the Antarctic Ocean – an Arctic Tern; from south and south-east Australia – Arctic and Common Terns, Manx Shearwater; southern (40°S) South America – Manx Shearwater; central (100°W) Canada – Mallard; and from the high Arctic in Greenland – Turnstone and Ringed Plover.

Ringing is only one tool in the study of bird migration. In recent years, radar observations have tended to dominate the scene, but even since the earliest years of *British Birds*, notes have regularly appeared on visual observations of migrant birds.

THE CONTINENTAL GOLDFINCH AS A BRITISH BIRD.

THE *Practical Handbook* records under this species : " Immigrant Goldfinches are recorded regularly from the east coast of England at the end of September and early November. Until actual specimens have been examined, however, the Continental form cannot be definitely included."

Some time ago I happened to get into conversation with A. B. Thompson of H.M.S. "Repulse." He told me that on November 1st, 1923, he opened the door of an unused boiler and out flew a Rook, and it immediately hid itself in the coal ! He went up on deck and found it " swarming with birds."

The following is the list of birds he remembered seeing :—
Rook, Hooded-Crow, Starling, Greenfinch, Goldfinch, Linnet,
Skylark, Thrush, Blackbird, Robin, Tit, Wren.

I got into communication with Rev. J. W. Evans and Lieut.-
Commander C. E. Morgan, R.N., and the latter kindly gave
me the following information. He remembered seeing the
birds mentioned in the list, except the Tit and Wren, and
added Sparrow, Jackdaw and Hawk. They all came on board
about 60 or 70 miles from shore between the Tyne and Flam-
borough Head, so that the Goldfinches were evidently on their
way to England. This fits in with the report on East Coast
migration (*Brit. Birds*, Vol. XVII., p. 262).

The Rooks came on board at about 3 p.m., the smaller birds
all that evening up till about 10 p.m. The Rooks mostly
roosted on the main-mast, and most of them left at 1 a.m.
The small birds were all over the ship, and many were still
about at 8 a.m. The wind on the 1st was easterly and very
light. " The Rooks flew alongside the ship for a long time
before they came on board, and were flying at the rate of about
17 to 18 miles per hour."   NORMAN H. JOY.

MIGRATION OF COMMON SCOTERS AND OTHER
DUCKS.

IN connection with the appearance of Common Scoters
(*Œdemia nigra*) in Hertfordshire, Buckinghamshire, and
Cheshire on April 10th, 1910 (Vol. III., pp. 414, 415) I may
note that on April 13th I witnessed an enormous migratory
movement of this species off Dungeness Point, Kent. As
soon as it was daylight flock after flock of these birds passed the
point coming from the west and flying east. This migration
lasted for at least two and a half hours, the flocks passing
almost without intermission the whole time, and had for the
most part finished by 8.30 a.m. So numerous were the birds
at the height of the migration that I counted thirty-two flocks
(from ten to sixty birds in a flock), passing the point in twenty
minutes. Besides Common Scoters I saw five flocks of Brent
Geese (*Bernicla brenta*), five single Divers and several small
parties of Terns (*Sterna fluviatilis* or *S. macrura*), all steadily
going eastwards. It would be interesting to know whether
these birds kept on eastwards or whether after passing the
Foreland they turned north.

On April 2nd in two different places in Romney Marsh,
Kent, there were masses of Mallard (*Anas boscas*), Wigeon
(*Mareca penelope*) and Teal (*Nettion crecca*), and in one place
some Tufted Duck (*Fuligula cristata*), Pochard (*F. ferina*),
Pintail (*Dafila acuta*) and many Shovelers (*Spatula clypeata*) ;
some had left in a day or two, and most had gone by the
16th. Garganey (*Querquedula circia*) had arrived by the 10th.

CLAUD B. TICEHURST.

MIGRATION IN JANUARY.

I DO not know whether other observers would agree that true migration appears to cease in this country about the beginning of December ; apart from local movements due to shortage of food, or larger movements obviously connected with a sudden spell of cold weather, I had never, until this winter, observed anything like real southward migration after about December 10th.

I was at Dungeness from December 30th, 1920 to January 3rd, 1921. December 31st was wet and stormy ; January 1st less windy, but very wet after 10 a.m. ; January 2nd wet and stormy ; and January 3rd sunny with hardly any wind. The temperature was well above the average all the time, and January 3rd would have done credit to the south of Italy. I believe similar mild conditions prevailed generally over our islands and the neighbouring parts of Europe. The shingle bushes, in which there are often a few Pipits and Linnets and other small birds, as well as Larks, in mid-winter, were exceptionally empty. I saw nothing but Larks in them.

At dawn on January 1st I rather thought I heard a Brambling's note, but as I did not hear it again I inferred that I had imagined it. Before sunrise on January 3rd a Meadow-Pipit (*Anthus pratensis*) came flying south along the shingle towards the point, and during the following hour or more (8—9 a.m.) small parties of Linnets (*Carduelis c. cannabina*) and a few Greenfinches (*Chloris c. chloris*) were frequently passing, flying in directions between south and west. A few of these seemed to have come in from the east, but they may only have been flying parallel to the coast a little way out, and come in at the point. Most of the morning I was on Littlestone sands, where I saw two Sky-Larks (*Alauda arvensis*) flying in from the east, but I could not be sure that they had not been feeding nearer the sea.

About 11.15 I saw a party of about fifteen Linnets flying steadily south over Littlestone sandhills. On my return to the point I specially crossed the ground on which Finches commonly settle, but I found none that had alighted. About 1.15 I heard a Goldfinch (*C. carduelis*) flying (apparently) west or south-west ; and a moment later two or three Linnets going in the same direction. Apparently this was about the end of the day's migration. In fact, the whole thing was just like a rather poor migration day in October or early November.

The birds I saw, as with nearly all the Finches I have seen migrating at Dungeness in autumn, were flying at an altitude that I estimated as about 100 feet, or rather less.

H. G. ALEXANDER.

Rare Birds at the Isle of May in 1911.—Miss E. V. Baxter and Miss L. J. Rintoul, to whose good work we have frequently referred, paid two visits to the Isle of May in 1911, viz. from April 27th to May 29th, and from September 8th to about October 6th. From their published results (*Scot. Nat.*, 1912, pp. 53-58) which are given in a most inconvenient narrative form, we extract the following interesting records:

Black Redstart (*Ruticilla titys*).—One, May 11th.

Continental Redbreast (*Erithacus rubecula rubecula*).— One, April 30th, the only Robin seen during the spring visit, while only British ones were seen in the autumn.

Lesser Whitethroat (*Sylvia curruca*).—Several, May 9th and May 15th.

Blackcap (*Sylvia atricapilla*).—A pair on November 15th.

Barred Warbler (*Sylvia nisoria*).—One, September 10th.

Continental Goldcrest (*Regulus cristatus cristatus*).— One, September 29th. Numbers of Goldcrests were seen during September, but all those procured except this one were of the British form, as were all those taken in the spring.

Northern Willow-Warbler (*Phylloscopus trochilus eversmanni*).—One, October 6th.

British Hedge-Sparrow (*Accentor modularis occidentalis*). —Some on September 30th, and a few on October 20th.

[I may here note that the British Hedge-Sparrow is a regular autumn-migrant on the south Yorkshire coast.—H.F.W.]

Red-backed Shrike (*Lanius collurio*).—A pair, May 11th.

Mealy Redpoll (*Linota linaria*).—One May 13th, one May 14th, two May 15th, and one May 29th.

Lapland Bunting (*Calcarius lapponicus*).—One September 28th, and one October 12th.

Rare Birds in Fair Isle.—Mr. W. Eagle Clarke contributes an interesting paper on the more uncommon visitors to Fair Isle during 1914 (*Scot. Nat.*, 1915, pp. 101–105). Mr. Jerome Wilson acted as regular observer—and apparently a very efficient one—during this year, while the Duchess of Bedford, who visited the island in the spring, added a valuable series of notes. We append below brief extracts of the more important records in this report, all being for the year 1914.

Northern Bullfinch (*Pyrrhula p. pyrrhula*).—Male and female February 27th, female February 28th.

Serin (*Serinus c. serinus*).—Female May 22nd. Only the second record for Scotland.

Ortolan Bunting (*Emberiza hortulana*).—An extraordinary number on May 8th.

Continental Great Titmouse (*Parus m. major*).—One on October 27th, followed by others to the number of about a dozen. Two stayed on at all events as late as January 23rd, 1915.

Siberian Chiffchaff (*Phylloscopus c. tristis*).—Female October 24th.

YELLOW-BROWED WARBLER (*Ph. s. superciliosus*).—One October 8th, one 28th.

REED-WARBLER (*Acrocephalus s. streperus*).—One June 10th. Previous records have been in autumn.

MARSH-WARBLER (*A. palustris*).—One June 8th. There are only three or four previous records for Scotland, and curiously the last was June 7th, 1913, at Fair Isle.

ICTERINE WARBLER (*Hypolais icterina*).—One June 11th.

BARRED WARBLER (*Sylvia n. nisoria*).—Appeared on ten different days between August 22nd and September 21st, as many as four being seen on August 29th.

BLACK REDSTART (*Phœnicurus o. gibraltariensis*).—Three times in April, once October.

HOBBY (*Falco s. subbuteo*).—One June 9th, and one November 21st.

WOOD-SANDPIPER (*Tringa glareola*).—Single birds on June 11th and 12th.

BLACK-TAILED GODWIT (*Limosa limosa*).—Two May 26th.

The places mentioned in these notes now form part of the network of Bird Observatories around the British coasts.

Other possibilities of deriving information from marked birds were quickly exploited – many are detailed elsewhere in this book. Return to the same nesting-site, and faithfulness to the same mate is one example; longevity another (see p129).

RETURN OF MARKED SWIFTS TO THEIR BREEDING PLACES.

SOME interesting results of the " ringing " of Swifts have recently appeared in the *Ornithologische Monatsberichte*, 1911, pp. 156, 168. Dr. Thienemann writes that on July 4th and 15th, 1910, Herr A. Gundlach of Neustrelitz, Mecklenburg, marked with rings two old Swifts (*Cypselus apus*) which were breeding in a Starling's nesting-box. At the beginning of July, 1911, the same birds were again found breeding in the same box. Ritter von Tschusi zu Schmidhoffen also states that in 1909 he succeeded in " ringing " a female Swift which was breeding under the eaves of a Starling's box, but failed to mark the male bird. In 1910 the " ringed " hen returned to the nesting place, and this time the male bird was also marked. On capturing the birds this season (1911), it was found that both male and female were the birds which had been marked in 1909 and 1910 respectively. One result of these observations is to show clearly that the rings have no injurious effect on the birds, for the female Swift " ringed " by Ritter von Tschusi has now worn the ring for three seasons without any ill effect. It would seem from these records that the Swift is a life-paired bird, returning to the same nesting place year after year.   F. C. R. JOURDAIN.

Longevity in Reed Warblers In 1964 I reported some remarkable cases of longevity in Reed Warblers *Acrocephalus scirpaceus* ringed and retrapped since 1951 at Jersey Bird Observatory (*Brit. Birds*, 57: 128-129). At that time we had records of a few individuals five or more years old, two aged at least nine, one eleven and one twelve. Two papers listing records of longevity in wild birds, as revealed by ringing, were cited but they showed an almost complete absence of small birds from their lists, the minimum age for inclusion being five years. We regarded the ages of the oldest Reed Warblers as so exceptional that they could not be truly representative of the maximum life-span of small passerines. There is now evidence, however, that such longevity is not so unusual. From the substantial body of data accumulated in the course of regular ringing in the colony of Reed Warblers adjoining the observatory, it appears that this species has a reasonable likelihood of attaining an age considerably greater than that usually accepted for small passerines. Up to August 1971, 392 (nearly 11% of the total ringed) had been retrapped a year or more after having been ringed. The longest intervals between ringing and retrapping are shown in the following table:

> 11 years: two birds, one ringed as an adult
> 10 years: three, one ringed as an adult
> 8 years: two, both ringed as adults
> 7 years: two
> 6 years: seven, two ringed as adults
> 5 years: 19, six ringed as adults
> 4 years: 32, twelve ringed as adults

Because those ringed as adults were at least a year old when ringed, one year should be added to the elapsed time to obtain their minimum ages.

I know of no comparable results from other colonies of Reed Warblers or for other small passerines, although there is absolutely no reason to think that in Jersey they are particularly long-lived; the accumulation of this long and continuous series of ringing/retrap data is due to the fortuitous siting, twenty years ago, of the observatory and its Heligoland trap on the edge of a breeding colony.   R. Long
Ornithological Section, Société Jersiaise, The Museum, St Helier, Jersey, Channel Islands

The phenomenal weight gains, due to stored fat, necessary to 'fuel' those migrants that may reach Africa non-stop on southward autumn migration are well documented for this Nightingale.

Large weight gain by migrant Nightingale   At Portland Bill, Dorset, Nightingales *Luscinia megarhynchos* occur annually in small numbers on spring and autumn passage. One caught at 18.55 BST on 27th August 1968 weighed 22.8 gm; it was retrapped on 29th and 30th, and on the latter date its weight was 22.7 gm, almost identical with that of three days earlier. It remained in the area, among dense brambles and blackthorn in a corner of the trapping garden of the bird observatory, and was seen on a number of occasions. It was again caught at 19.30 BST on 2nd September when it weighed 25.2 gm, an increase of 10.5% after six days (or 11.0% after only three days). It was then trapped for the fifth and last time at 16.00 BST on 11th September, by which time its weight had risen to an astonishing 34.8 gm (double-checked by an independent observer), an increase of 52.6% on the original figure of 15 days previously. A second Nightingale, first caught on 26th August 1968 and also trapped on 2nd September, had increased from 20.85 to 23.1 gm in the seven days, a gain of 10.8% which was very similar to that of the first individual at the same period; unfortunately, this second one was not caught subsequently. It may be added that the weights of 15 Nightingales trapped on arrival at Portland in *spring* in recent years have ranged from 17.95 to 23.25 gm, with a mean of 21.4 gm.   F. R. Clafton

Finally, ringers themselves were tempted to start devising their own experiments.

A GREENFINCH "HOMING" EXPERIMENT.

In the early part of 1934 I had the good fortune to catch a " homing " Greenfinch (*Chloris ch. chloris*) in my trap at Birmingham, which allowed me to carry out some interesting tests.

The Greenfinch, FL.423, was first trapped on January 26th as an adult male. It next visited the trap on the 31st, after which it came in every day. On February 7th I decided that it must be deported and on that day I took it one mile to the N.N.W., following this up by journeys of two, three and four miles in the same direction on the next three days. It took exactly two hours to do the return journey on the last occasion. On the fifth day it was taken two miles into the city to the N.E., and as I found it back in the trap when I returned two hours later, I promptly took it out five miles to the S.W. The first five journeys were all in urban areas ; this sixth one was out into the country. The bird was back in two and a half hours ! After this, stern measures had to be taken. Two days later the Greenfinch was deported seven miles to the south and returned in twenty-two hours. We gave him one day's rest and then took him ten and a quarter miles S.E., only to see him back in the trap forty-three hours later. For the next few days he returned to the trap as fast as we threw him out, so on February 22nd I again took him ten and a quarter miles, but this time to the W.S.W. Here he was cut off from the trap by the Clent Hills which rise to about a thousand feet at their highest point—some 600 feet above the point of the bird's release. The Greenfinch was not seen again until March 7th, thirteen days later. For the rest of March the bird was constantly in and out of the trap, but in April his visits were less frequent, and he was last seen on the 22nd, and two days later trapping ceased for the season.

There are a few more details which, I think, may be of interest. The trap is an ordinary " house trap " in a field about seventy yards from the house, which is on the S.W. side of Birmingham, with a belt of fields leading out into the country to the west. The food put in the trap is usually shredded suet, No. 1 Chick Food, and sometimes household scraps. On journey No. 2, two miles N.N.W., the bird was accompanied by another cock Greenfinch, FL.422 ; they returned together. On journeys Nos. 1-6, the bird was released in the morning, but for 7-9 at 6.30 in the evening, when it was dark. Further, after he had been released on February 22nd there followed several days of fog in the district which, I think, was partly responsible for the long time which elapsed between the release and the return.

Finally, I am glad to say that he visited the trap again on December 12th, to show that he was still alive, and though he has not appeared since, I am hoping to see him again in the spring. W. E. KENRICK.

Perhaps the most remarkable homing experiment of all involved a Manx Shearwater, taken from its breeding burrow on Skokholm, off Pembrokeshire, and conveyed in a box by various means (including a trans-Atlantic aircraft) to Boston, USA, and released there. It navigated home across the featureless Atlantic in twelve days, reaching its burrow before details of its release reached the island!

✦ 6 ✦

Goings and Comings

The wording of this chapter title is deliberately reversed from normal usage. Over the last couple of decades, in particular, public environmental interest has been at its height and most views on the fate of wildlife have been fashionably gloomy. We hear of many species of animals and birds on the brink of extinction, often because of man's expansionism or his thoughtless production of toxic pollutants. The broader view indicates that although in many cases there *is* a very real cause for concern, there are also considerable gains which tend to receive much less comment.

The pages of *British Birds* generally support this optimistic view and seldom mention declining species.

EXTERMINATION OF THE SEA-EAGLE
IN IRELAND.

IN the *Zoologist*, 1911 (p. 346). Mr. R. Warren records the disappearance of the Sea-Eagles (*Haliaëtus albicilla*) from their last breeding haunts in Ireland, on the cliffs of north Mayo. They have been destroyed by the keepers of the adjacent grouse-shootings, and at the present time the only relics of their former presence are the old nests, which are still visible at several places along the cliffs. Mr. Warren mentions one on the great cliff of Loughtmuriga, another on

Alt More, and three on the great cliff of Alt Redmond, besides one on Spinks : the five last named being situated on the range of cliffs between Porturlin and Portacloy. On July 1st, 1892, Mr. Warren was fortunate enough to see one of these Eagles with a hare in its talons, pursued by an angry Peregrine, and in all probability on its way to the nest. During the two following years the Eagles were reported to be present as usual on the cliffs, but no one seems to have seen an occupied nest. In May, 1898, in company with Messrs. Ussher and Howard Saunders, evidence of the presence of these birds was found in the shape of an eagle's feather, and the skeleton of a hare which must have been killed within a week or two. In August of the present year Messrs. Warren and Barrington revisited the north Mayo coast and rowed along the base of the cliffs, but could find no traces of the Eagles, while the boatmen all agreed that it was some years since any had been observed in their old haunts.

The disappearance of this fine species from the Irish fauna is a national loss, and is the more to be regretted as the breeding stock in Scotland is now reduced to a very low ebb, so that any untoward accident to the few surviving pairs will mean the extinction of this species in the British Isles. Mr. Warren is of opinion that the Golden Eagle (*Aquila chrysaëtus*) is in Ireland on the verge of extermination, being reduced to a single pair, and states that the eyrie on Muilrea is now unoccupied, the last bird having been poisoned in the spring of 1910. Possibly in this case the number of surviving birds may be under-estimated.   F. C. R. JOURDAIN.

The spectacular Sea Eagle is the subject of a recolonisation experiment, being carried out on the island of Rhum by the Nature Conservancy Council. Young birds, expatriated from parts of northern Europe where persecution is still the rule, seem, at the time of writing, to be settling in western Scotland, and the early stages of display, which leads to pair formation, have been watched.

An equally cheerful picture cannot be composed for the Corncrake. These two notes in themselves report a *status quo*, but, reading between the lines, concern is already apparent.

LAND-RAILS IN STAFFORDSHIRE.

I AM pleased to report that the Land-Rail (*Crex crex*) turned up this year in quite average numbers in the district of Cheadle, Staffordshire. On May 9th, 1915, one was killed close to the town of Longton by flying against telegraph-wires. This very dry season is bringing on a very early hay harvest, and this will be most disastrous to Land-Rails' nests, which will be mown over and destroyed before the young are hatched. This result will probably cause a diminished number of this waning species.   J. MASEFIELD.

STATUS OF CORN-CRAKE IN GLOUCESTERSHIRE.

WITH reference to the recent " Report on the Distribution and Status of the Corn-Crake (*Crex crex*) " (*antea*, pp. 142-148, 162-168), it may be of interest to record the following :

In June, 1942, I was walking down the side of the Severn in Gloucestershire with a man who lives on the river bank and has quite a good knowledge of birds, and we located seven Corn-Crakes in a distance of perhaps five miles. In one case my companion's dog brought an egg to us in his mouth and in another a dead young bird. His owner told me that this happens every year and he is unable to prevent the dog doing it. I was near Gloucester again in 1943 and I could hear the birds all along the river in the hayfields ; the first one I heard was almost within the city limits. The person I was with regularly walks the river bank in connexion with his work and he considered the birds still common there.

To my knowledge the Corn-Crake breeds in three different localities just inside the Radnorshire border. A. W. BOLT.

This concern is well founded: the ever-diminishing Corncrake population is now almost entirely restricted to the Scottish islands and Ireland. Thus the Corncrake joins the Wryneck and the Red-backed Shrike on the short list of Britain and Ireland's vanishing birds.

Turning to the more cheerful side, the British Isles are now so well explored (particularly since the British Trust for Ornithology's *Atlas* project) that it is difficult to envisage a note of this nature today.

A NEW NESTING-PLACE OF THE GANNET.

WHEN looking northward from Hermaness Hill, Unst, this month, July 1920, I noticed a number of Gannets (*Sula bassana*) nesting on the big " stack " to the west of Muckle Flugga. I was with Henry Edwardson at the time, and he told me he had noticed some there last year. There seemed to be about 100 pairs on the south side of the " stack " : we could not see the north side. This " stack " is called the " Rumblings." There appeared to be another smaller colony on a " stack " farther to the west, but they were on the north side, and we could only occasionally see the birds rise above the edge of the cliff. This " stack " appears to be called " Humla Stack." Mr. Edwardson, who has spent the summer in his little hut on this remote hill for thirty-one years, says he is certain that Gannets never nested here before during his years of watching. These two colonies, with the small colony on Noss, now of ten pairs, which first appeared in 1915, should in time largely help the Gannet population of the world.   E. G. B. MEADE-WALDO.

It is easy to imagine the thrill of delight in such a remote spot! It is also difficult today to remember that gulls inland were once – until relatively recently – a noteworthy oddity.

GREAT BLACK-BACKED GULLS IN LONDON.

THE somewhat unusual occurrence of a party of seven adult Great Black-backed Gulls (*Larus marinus*) on the river at Westminster on the morning of April 14th, 1924, may be worth recording. I first saw them a little before high-water when they were the only Gulls in view on that stretch of the river. They remained soaring, wheeling, and dipping for floating morsels of food, between Lambeth and Vauxhall bridges, till an hour or more after the turn of the tide, then disappeared. A southerly gale had been blowing during the night.   H. A. F. MAGRATH.

Of greater interest today is the increasing number of the more exciting northern gulls.

Glaucous and Iceland Gulls in the west midlands The increasing tendency of the commoner species of gull to winter inland has been well documented (see, for example, *Bird Study*, 1 : 129-148;

14: 104-113). Most publications, however, still describe the Glaucous Gull *Larus hyperboreus* and the Iceland Gull *L. glaucoides* as exceptional inland, except in the London area. Recent experience in the west midlands, particularly at the larger Staffordshire reservoirs, indicates that both these species are in fact regular visitors to large inland gull roosts. Up to and including the winter of 1974/75, 65 Glaucous Gulls and 50 Iceland were recorded in the old counties of Warwickshire, Worcestershire and Staffordshire (including the now separate county of West Midlands), 83% of them since 1968/69. During the course of a single winter as many as eleven Glaucous and eight Iceland Gulls have been identified, and on 11th February 1973 no fewer than three Iceland Gulls were recorded together at Blithfield Reservoir, Staffordshire.

Table 1. Records of Glaucous Gulls *Larus hyperboreus* **and Iceland Gulls** *L. glaucoides* **in the old counties of Warwickshire, Worcestershire and Staffordshire**
Figures for the winter of 1974/75 are provisional

		pre-1966	WINTER 66/67	67/68	68/69	69/70	70/71	71/72	72/73	73/74	74/75	TOTALS
Glaucous Gull	adult	1	0	0	0	4	1	4	3	3	3	19
	immature	9	1	2	5	5	6	7	4	4	3	46
	TOTALS	10	1	2	5	9	7	11	7	7	6	65
Iceland Gull	adult	0	0	0	0	2	3	4	5	4	5	23
	immature	6	0	1	1	5	4	4	3	2	1	27
	TOTALS	6	0	1	1	7	7	8	8	6	6	50

All the known records in the three counties are summarised in table 1, adult and immature birds being shown separately. The totals should be regarded as minima, since allowance has been made for the possibility of a single individual making several appearances at the same or neighbouring roosts during the course of a winter. The monthly distribution of records is given in table 2.

Table 2. Monthly distribution of the records summarised in table 1 above

	Oct	Nov	Dec	Jan	Feb	Mar	Apr	May
Glaucous Gull	2	3	14	10	18	15	3	0
Iceland Gull	0	1	7	12	12	15	2	1

It is evident from these figures that since the late 1960's both species have been of regular occurrence, Glaucous generally appearing between December and March and Iceland between late December and March. The total number of birds is not large but, nonetheless, compares favourably with many coastal areas of similar latitude.

An interesting feature of the records is the high percentage of adults involved, particularly in the case of the Iceland Gull. Taking all records into account, 29% of Glaucous and 46% of Iceland were adults; considering only those occurrences since 1969/70 (77% of all records), these figures become 38% and 52% respectively. According to the literature, adult birds of both species are relatively sedentary and rarely move very far south. The increasing proportion of adults in the west midlands may therefore presage a change in the wintering habits of these two species and it will be interesting to see if this trend is maintained.

ALAN R. DEAN and BRIAN R. DEAN
2 Charingworth Road, Solihull, West Midlands B92 8HT

The case of the Fulmar (or Fulmar Petrel of early volumes) is particularly well-documented – perhaps partly because of James Fisher's enthusiasm – and of great biological fascination. The history is largely self-explanatory, and is perhaps best begun with Harvie-Brown's summary of 1913.

THE DISTRIBUTION OF THE FULMAR PETREL.

IN our last volume a number of interesting notes were published relating to the extraordinary extension of the breeding-range of the Fulmar (*Fulmarus g. glacialis*) in recent years. Mr J. A. Harvie-Brown has just contributed a valuable paper on the subject (*Scot. Nat.*, 1912, pp. 97-102 and 121-32 and map) in which he traces in detail the extension of its breeding-range. Mr. Harvie-Brown draws attention to two important facts : (1) the Fulmar established itself in the Færoes as comparatively recently as about 1839 ; (2) the St. Kilda colony dates back at least two hundred and fifty years.

The following is a list of the places and first dates at which nesting was observed, extracted from Mr. Harvie-Brown's paper :—

SHETLANDS.

1878 (or previous) Foula.
1891 Horn of Papa off Papa Stour.
1896 (or 1895) Calder's Geo, Eshaness (Mainland).
1897 Hermaness (Unst).
1897 Ramna Stacks (north Mainland).
1898 Noup of Noss near Lerwick.
1900 Fitful Head, south of Mainland.
1901 Noup o' Norby, Sandness.
1902 Uyea Cliffs and other points north-west Mainland.
1906 Whalsey and Yell.
1908 Bressay and possibly Hascosay.

FAIR ISLE.

1903 (or previous).

ORKNEYS.

1900 (or previous) Hoy Head.
1901 Westray.
1907 Between Stromness and Bay of Skaill.
1910 Markwick Head.
1911 Deerness and Copinshay.

MAINLAND.

1897 Clomore Cliffs (Cape Wrath) (Sutherland).
1900 Dunnet Head (north Caithness).
1911 Berriedale Head (east Caithness).

HANDA (west coast Sutherland).

1902

HEBRIDES.

St. Kilda original British colony.
1886 North Rona.
1887 Sulisgeir.
1902 (probably earlier) Flannan Isles.
1902 (probably earlier) Barra Head.
1904 Eilean Mor.
1910 Shiant Isles (no doubt nesting but nests not seen).

IRELAND.

1911 (possibly 1907) north Mayo coast.
1911 (probably 1910) Ulster coast.

The subsequent southward spread was relatively slow and unsteady – not least because the birds often 'prospected' suitable cliffs for some years before breeding.

FULMARS BREEDING ON THE FARNE ISLANDS.—Fulmar Petrels (*Fulmarus g. glacialis*) were first seen haunting the Farne Islands in summer in 1919. Mr. F. H. Edmondson states (*Nat.*, 1935, p. 231) that the bird definitely bred there in 1935 and that this is the first season either an egg has been seen or the young have hatched. The late G. Bolam, in his *Catalogue of the Birds of Northumberland* (1932, p. 147), states, however, that " it was not until 1929 that any definite information of their actual breeding there was forthcoming". Perhaps Mr. Edmondson has overlooked this statement.

FULMAR PETRELS BREEDING IN PEMBROKESHIRE.

WITH reference to my note on the Fulmar Petrels (*Fulmarus g. glacialis*) probably breeding at the Stack Rocks in 1935, (Vol. XXIX, p. 117) the coastguard informs me quite definitely that in 1935 one egg was laid by a pair. He was, however, unable to say whether the egg hatched or not.

I visited the colony on June 22nd, 1936, and I saw five pairs in view at one time and I think that the number of Fulmars is greater than in June, 1935. Moreover, one pair has extended the range and now occupies a ledge in the next small bay. I saw no eggs, however. W. A. CADMAN.

NESTING OF FULMAR PETREL ON THE BASS ROCK AND INCUBATION PERIOD.

ALTHOUGH several Fulmar Petrels (*Fulmarus g. glacialis*) have frequented the Bass Rock for three or four springs, it was not until last year (1936) that an egg was laid. It disappeared and was probably destroyed by Herring-Gulls. This year (1937) two pairs laid, but in one case the egg disappeared. In the other the egg was laid on May 26th and hatched on July 9th, making an incubation period of 44 days, as compared with 40 to 41 days in the case of an Orkney bird recorded by me in these pages (Vol. XXX, p. 194). Unfortunately the nestling period of the Bass Rock bird could not be taken for comparison, as the chick perished by falling out of the nest on to a ledge about 18 feet below. H. W. ROBINSON.

[There are considerable discrepancies in the observed incubation periods of the species. Recent observations by R. Richter give a period of 57 days in one case and between 55 and 57 days in another.—F.C.R.J.]

FIRST SUCCESSFUL BREEDING OF THE
FULMAR IN ISLE OF MAN.

FOLLOWING the first record of definite breeding of the Fulmar (*Fulmarus g. glacialis*) in Cumberland (*antea*, p. 61) this year (1941) also saw the first successful breeding of the species in the Isle of Man.

Previously no eggs had ever been found on the coast of the Island (although an egg was seen on the Calf in 1936). This year a careful count at Kione ny Ghoggan revealed 12 pairs in May and no fewer than four of these laid eggs although two pairs deserted before the eggs hatched. On July 22nd the writers found a young Fulmar on a ledge and a second was found here on August 3rd. On August 14th, Mr. and Mrs. W. S. Kennedy and W. S. Cowin also found a well-grown Fulmar at the Castle Rocks. All three birds were closely watched until they left the ledges, the last being seen there on August 31st and there can be no doubt all three were successfully reared. This is the first time that successful breeding has been proved in the Isle of Man.

W. S. COWIN AND B.R.S. AND E. M. MEGAW.

FULMARS IN SUMMER IN DORSET.

ON May 12th, 1943, two Fulmar Petrels (*Fulmarus g. glacialis*) were seen flying up and down a stretch of the Dorset coast and occasionally visiting a third which sat on a ledge near the top of the cliffs. On June 8th and 24th a single bird was seen in exactly the same place and it is possible that a second bird was present on both these occasions, for the bird which I was watching alighted on a part of the cliff-face that it was impossible to inspect.

G. BERNARD GOOCH.

[This appears to be the first evidence of the presence of Fulmars on the south coast of England in summer, though it does not give proof of breeding.—EDS.]

FIRST BREEDING OF FULMAR IN THE SOUTH-WEST.

THE first Fulmar (*Fulmarus g. glacialis*) ever recorded in the breeding season at Lundy Island, off the Devon coast, was one that flew past the North Landing on June 11th, 1922 (Loyd, *antea*, Vol. xvi, p. 155). This bird showed no sign of being "interested" in the cliffs; and Fulmars were not seen regularly about them until the summer of 1935 (Perry, *Lundy, Isle of Puffins*, 1940). In 1939 Fulmars were seen about the Lundy cliffs from April 12th to July 10th (Perry, *l.c.*); the greatest number of individuals seen was nine (June 13th) and up to four sites were occupied, though breeding did not take place.

In 1944, on a date before May 21st, Mr. F. W. Gade informs us, a Fulmar at Lundy Island laid the first egg ever to have been seen in the south-west. Shortly after it was laid the egg was taken, in ignorance, by a temporary resident of the island. Three pairs were present in occupation of sites and it was thought that another oı these was also incubating, in an inaccessible place. At the end of July, four empty " nest-sites," or scrapes, were found on a thorough examination of the cliff with the use of a rope. The Fulmars had by this time entirely disappeared (as is often the case at a station where Fulmars are simply " prospecting " or have made an unsuccessful attempt at breeding) and there was no evidence that any other eggs had been laid. One adult Fulmar returned and was seen at the cliff on August 3rd.

Fulmars have been present for a long time, in the breeding season, at south-west cliffs. Though the above is the first and only record of breeding, birds have been present at the Scillies since 1937 (Ryves and Valentine, *Rep. Cornwall Bird Watching and Preservn. Soc.*, 1937) ; on the Cornish mainland since 1936 (Boyd, communication to B.T.O. inquiry) (Land's End first, now several other places on the north coast) ; on the South Devon mainland since 1943 (Fisher, *antea*, Vol. xxxvii, p. 140) (Start Point) ; on Dorset cliffs since 1943 (Gooch, *antea*, Vol. xxxvii, p. 98) ; at the cliffs of the Isle of Wight since 1942 (Fisher, *l.c.*) ; and in South Wales, at Skokholm since 1931 (Lockley, communication to B.T.O. inquiry) ; and the Pembrokeshire mainland since 1931 (Lloyd, *antea*, Vol. xxv, pp. 81-2).

The British Trust for Ornithology is continuing its Inquiry into the distribution and spread of the Fulmar, and particulars can be obtained from J. Fisher at 39, Museum Road, Oxford.

MARTIN COLES HARMAN.
JAMES FISHER.

The coast of Britain is now completely ringed with Fulmar breeding stations. Even in those areas apparently inappropriate for cliff-nesting species, like the Dungeness shingle peninsula in Kent, birds are considering 'ledges' on the nuclear power stations as suitable replicas of their natural surroundings. All this seems more amazing when the long adolescence of the Fulmar (about eight years) and the single-egg-per-annum rate of reproduction are taken into account. Perhaps the remarkable spread is best accounted for by the basic adaptability of the bird, and by the length of its life. Many Fulmars outlive the rings placed on their legs, and it is thought that a significant proportion live for twenty years or more – easily offsetting their low reproductive rate.

There has been a flurry of breeding 'invaders' from continental Europe since the 1930s. One of the first among these is so common in many European towns that its absence from southern Britain was remarkable; the Black Redstart chose war-stricken London in which to hit the headlines.

BLACK REDSTART IN LONDON IN MAY AND JUNE.

On May 20th, 1939, I heard a Black Redstart (*Phœnicurus o. gibraltariensis*) singing on the tower of the University of London building in Bloomsbury. The porter told me that the bird had begun singing about a week before. It continued to sing irregularly till June 22nd, being silent for periods up to a week in length ; I heard it at most times of the day on different occasions. It would perch on some corner of the tower, sometimes even on the flagpole (270 ft.), or on the King Edward VII wing of the British Museum. On June 17th I saw it fly down from the north-east corner of the British Museum wing, where it had been singing, to the waste excavated area east of the University building, adjoining Montague Place. After a few minutes' activity, apparently in searching for food, it flew back and sang again for about half an hour. It repeated this performance several times, and with Mr. A. Holte Macpherson and others I was able to observe it closely on the ground. It was a one-year-old male, having no white on its wing. Neither then nor at any other time was a female seen, and it was clear then from its behaviour that it was alone. It was not heard or seen after June 22nd.

J. LE C. SUMNER.

Hostilities had begun in earnest when breeding was proved, and subsequently many pairs, doubtless reminded of their original mountain scree habitat, took advantage of the devastated buildings and rubble in the blitzed areas of the City to secrete their nests.

BLACK REDSTART BREEDING IN INNER LONDON.

In April, 1940, Miss M. I. Tetley saw a pair of Redstarts in the very secluded Little Cloister, Westminster Abbey, where she was staying. She noticed that the tail of one was of a brighter red than that of the other and assumed at the time that the birds were of the species with which she was familiar at her home in Windermere. Hearing of this a few weeks later, I made inquiries and ascertained that the birds were still frequenting the Abbey, and after investigating the buildings in the neighbourhood, on May 13th I found a Black Redstart (*Phœnicurus o. gibraltariensis*) in full adult dress singing on a house a few yards from the Cloisters.

I failed to see the hen, and feared she might have fallen prey to a Kestrel which often perches on a neighbouring pinnacle of the Abbey. On June 2nd, however, Miss Tetley wrote that she had just seen what she believed were two young Black Redstarts on the lawn of the old Abbey Garden, which she had kindly obtained leave for me to visit ; and there on June 4th I found two Black Redstarts hawking flies from the top of a lawn tennis net like Spotted Flycatchers. One was clearly a young bird. I watched it through field glasses at close range for half an hour during which it was most active. The other, which did not remain long, gave me the impression of being very slightly greyer on the mantle and was, I expect, the female parent.

The Abbey is not more than 300 yards from Marsham Street, where Mr. E. M. Nicholson discovered a Black Redstart in the summer of 1936 (*antea*, Vol. XXX., p. 320).

It would be interesting to know how many Black Redstarts are in London this summer. Since the middle of May I have been receiving reports of Black Redstarts seen singing on prominent buildings in the Westminster district ; one as far from the Abbey as Berkeley Square. These were possibly all the Abbey bird. But one which has frequented the Natural History Museum since May 30th is certainly another ; and so probably is one seen and heard singing by Dr. P. Manson-Bahr a few weeks ago on one of the buildings of the White City. A. HOLTE MACPHERSON.

BLACK REDSTARTS IN INNER LONDON.

IT is clear from comparing the dates at which they were seen and heard that several Black Redstarts (*Phœnicurus o. gibraltariensis*) have spent the summer in Inner London.

Apart from the birds which bred at Westminster Abbey (*antea*, p. 46) there was (1) a male bird whose headquarters was St. James's Church, Piccadilly. It was seen and heard singing regularly on the church and neighbouring buildings and was probably the same bird as was noticed more than once in St. James's Street, Berkeley Square and Farm Street. This bird was seen by Sir Cyril Hurcomb, Mr. E. M. Nicholson and almost daily by Mr. G. W. Collett, who tells me it left the church after June 21st being apparently disturbed by the building of an air-raid shelter in the churchyard. (2) Another male regularly frequented St. Martin's-in-the-Fields often visiting the National Gallery and other large buildings in the vicinity. I received reports of it from Miss M. S. van Oostveen, Mr. R. S. R. Fitter, Mr. R. A. Richardson and Mr. A. V. Tucker. (3) Another established itself at the Natural History Museum, South Kensington at the end of May. It was first identified by Mr. A. H. Bishop and could be seen and heard singing on the roof and towers for several weeks. It is possible that this is the bird identified by Dr. P. Manson-Bahr at the White City (just outside Inner London) the day before one was seen at the Museum.

I suspect that there was also another male in the district immediately south of Westminster Abbey, for Miss M. I. Tetley on several occasions saw and heard one singing on St. John's Church, Smith's Square ; once, when she had just left one singing in the Abbey garden, where on June 30th she saw two singing at the same time.

Except in the case of the Abbey pair, there is no satisfactory evidence of the presence of a female Black Redstart.

I have reason to think that the Abbey pair reared more than one young, but circumstances have made thorough investigation impossible. It will be noticed that these birds have all been recorded from Westminster or Kensington, a very limited area, and at a time when many London ornithologists were absent on war service. The inference that other Black Redstarts probably escaped notice is obvious.

A. HOLTE MACPHERSON.

BLACK REDSTARTS IN ENGLAND IN SUMMER.

IN 1942 Black Redstarts have been reported in summer in London, Cambridgeshire, Kent, Devon, Suffolk, Sussex and Yorkshire. The great increase both in the area from which they have been reported and in the numbers present—upwards of 20 were observed in London alone—suggests that they have occurred also in other places which have not yet come to our notice.

To trace the spreading of this bird year by year is a matter of great interest and we are anxious to compile as complete a record

as possible. We shall therefore be grateful for information not hitherto sent to us or published in these pages of Black Redstarts seen in the British Isles between the months of April and August in 1942 or previous years, indicating date, nature of locality, numbers present, sexes where known, and whether breeding occurred. Breeding localities will of course be treated in strict confidence if desired. Letters can be addressed to either of us at 326, High Holborn, London, W.C.1.

H. F. WITHERBY, R. S. R. FITTER.

Interestingly, perhaps due to the desirability of keeping the extent of damage to the capital city secret in wartime, nesting sites are mentioned only in barest detail. By 1943, breeding was widespread, although the numbers involved were small.

BLACK REDSTARTS IN ENGLAND IN THE SUMMER OF 1943

BY

R. S. R. FITTER.

IN the summer of 1943 Black Redstarts (*Phœnicurus ochrurus gibraltariensis*) were present in eleven English counties, and nested in five of them ; in 1942 they had been present in nine counties and nested in five. In 1943 no reports were received of Black Redstarts in Devon or Yorkshire, as in 1942, but first breeding records for Suffolk and Warwickshire were received. Altogether at least ten pairs nested in England in 1943, compared with six in 1942, and five pairs successfully reared second broods. It seems certain that the bird is still extending its range, and but for the restrictions on observation due to the war many more would probably have been reported. It is desirable that as soon as military conditions make it possible, all the towns on the south and east coasts of England should be thoroughly searched for Black Redstarts.

Retrospective information has come to light on the breeding of a few pairs, in Middlesex since 1926, and in Sussex on and off since 1909. Recent changes have been only of degree: Black Redstarts increase and decrease from area to area, occasionally exploiting new habitats like power stations or tower blocks, or 'new town' centres, but as yet show few signs of anything but a tenuous hold as breeding birds.

A beneficiary of the post-war explosion of building and rebuilding was the Little Ringed Plover. Clay, chalk, sand and ballast extraction pits suited the birds well.

THE LITTLE RINGED PLOVER IN THE LONDON AREA IN 1947

BY

E. R. PARRINDER.

IN 1947 Little Ringed Plovers (*Charadrius dubius curonicus*) bred in the London Area for the fourth year in succession, and there was a remarkable increase in numbers. Eight nests were found and four other broods seen. Because of the possibility that at least two pairs changed their sites after disturbance the exact number present is unknown, but there were certainly eleven and possibly fourteen pairs. Although the majority of the birds were again in Middlesex there was an extension of range to three other counties, and first breeding records were obtained for Essex (four pairs), Kent and Berkshire (one pair each). It is probable that the apparent sudden increase, from four pairs in 1946 to a minimum of eleven pairs in 1947, is in part due to a lack of observation in previous years. The Essex site, in particular, was visited for the first time in 1947, when four well-established pairs were found, and it seems likely that Little Ringed Plovers may have bred at this site, unobserved, for some years. It is curious that the known breeding range of the species in Britain is, so far, restricted to Tring (where it bred in 1938 and 1944) and the London Area (where it has bred annually since 1944) and one wonders how far this restriction is due to a lack of observation in other suitable places. In the London Area the gravel pits, of which there are nearly two hundred, are the chief habitat, and the essential factors appear to be a reasonably undisturbed flat area of gravel, shingle or stony soil for nesting, in close association with water with a sand or mud edge, for feeding. These conditions are usually found in pits which are being worked, but the state of a pit may change rapidly and it may become unsuitable in the following year, or even in the same season, by a change in the water level or by becoming overgrown.

A decade later, the invasion had spread as far as the north of England.

Little Ringed Plover breeding In Cheshire.—On 23rd June 1954 I found 4 Little Ringed Plovers (*Charadrius dubius*) at a locality in central Cheshire adjacent to some shallow pools. The following day A. W. Boyd accompanied me to the place and we saw the 4 birds again. As they were observed simultaneously only in flight, we were not certain whether all the individuals were adults or whether any young birds were present. Those watched on the ground, however, were on each occasion adults.

A single bird was seen on 2nd July, after which date no further visits were made until 13th July when I found a bird sitting on a nest containing four eggs. The nest was situated within four feet of the water's edge and had not been in existence at the time of the earlier visits. Boyd saw the sitting bird on the next day and the eggs were still in the nest on the 18th, but no Little Ringed Plovers other than the sitting bird were seen. On 24th July, however, the eggs had gone and a thorough search of the area on this and the following day showed no sign of any adults or young birds.

In view of the lateness in the season when the eggs were laid it is possible that this was a second nest. It was noted that the water level rose considerably following periods of heavy rain and some suitable nesting areas were submerged, and this could easily have accounted for an earlier failure. The eggs from the nest that was found were, however, not lost in this way and an avian or rodent predator was suspected. This is the second recorded occurrence of the species in the county and the first attempt at breeding.   E. L. ARNOLD

Little Ringed Plovers breeding in Nottinghamshire.—Two nests of Little Ringed Plover (*Charadrius dubius*), each containing a clutch of four eggs, were found at a gravel-pit in the Trent Valley in 1956; the first nest was discovered by A. Teather on 24th June, the second was confirmed by W. Priestley on 2nd July. The first clutch disappeared when near hatching; the second produced four chicks of which only one survived the very wet weather. Observations showed that two pairs were present. These are the first breeding records for the county.

A third pair took up territory at another gravel-pit some 30 miles away and were seen by W. Priestley to be making scrapes on 13th May. These birds were present throughout the summer and, although no young were observed, the adults' behaviour suggested their presence, especially during July. A. Dobbs

[As we have stated previously, we are publishing separate records of Little Ringed Plovers breeding only when a new county is involved and, although 1956 seems to have been a year of very successful consolidation in some parts of the country, Nottinghamshire is the only new colonisation of which we have heard. This year is the third since Mr. E. R. Parrinder's previous three-year summary of the spread of this species, and we are glad to be able to announce that he has agreed to prepare for us an analysis for 1954-56, which we hope to publish as early as possible in 1957.—Eds.]

Now there are Scottish breeding areas, and in the south even the temporary excavations accompanying new roads are quickly colonised – if only for a year or two – by this adaptable bird.

Who, reading the note below in 1957, could have believed that the Collared Dove would be where it is today?

Collared Dove in Surrey.—On 15th April 1956, at Gomshall, Surrey, I found a dove with a dark half-collar; and subsequently, on the 29th, I identified it as a Collared Dove (*Streptopelia decaocto*) by means of the darker primaries compared with the general coloration of the back. Later visits to the area were paid in the company of Dr. W. Rees-Thomas and family, and Mr. P. Holness; the bird, which was considered from its behaviour to be a male, was then seen at much closer range and also heard calling. Mr. D. Freshwater observed it as well, on another occasion.

Initially, I found field-identification difficult because of the effects of shadows cast by twigs, and it was necessary to see the bird side-on in a good light in order to distinguish the primaries.

When I obtained an extremely good view with a telescope at a
range of some 20 feet, I could see that the edges of the primaries
were abraded, so that the true colour was not always clear. There
was no doubt that they were darker than the general coloration of
the rest of the wings and the back, although I would not describe
this feature as conspicuous. The pinkish tinge to the breast was
also visible when the bird was close at hand, but was not obvious
in a normal view, particularly against the sky. The bird had
struck me as, differing from the domesticated Barbary Dove (*S.
risoria*), not only on these features, but also on first impression
because of the greyer colour of its back, an impression that was
strengthened during later visits. The eyes looked dark and even
through a telescope I could not observe the red colour referred to
in the *Field-Guide*. Dr. Rees-Thomas, however, caught a glint of
red when a ray of sunlight momentarily fell on one of the eyes.
The bill was dark, and the legs were pink and unadorned with any
form of ring.

The typical call of the species, "coo-coooo-cuk", with the
accent on the second syllable, was unmistakable, although
occasionally the hard "c" of the coo was softened to a guttural
"chroo-chrooo-cuk". A flight-call consisting of a sort of low-
pitched shriek (my rendering was "hurrrr") was also heard.

The bird paid regular visits to feed in a chicken-run in the
garden of a local house, and Mr. V. H. Lacey, the occupant, stated
that the bird had been observed there since 6th April.
Dr. Rees-Thomas took advantage of this feeding-habit to obtain
a colour photograph by using one of the hen-coops as a hide. The
bird was last observed on 13th May by which time it had taken
territorial possession of an elm, was in full song and disputed the

right of other species—Mistle Thrush (*Turdus viscivorus*), for example—to use the tree. The aggressive display consisted of inflating the crop, lowering and spreading the tail, and calling loudly when approaching the intruder. G. H. FORSTER

[There can be no reasonable doubt now that the Collared Dove has reached this country as a wild immigrant from the Continent (see pp. 239-246), but as some of this species were imported by at least two dealers in the early 1950's, though not apparently since 1952 (*antea*, vol. xlvi, p. 55; and vol. xlix, pp. 345-346), there must remain a possibility that isolated occurrences like that described above refer to captive birds that have escaped. It should be added that Dr. Rees-Thomas's photograph mentioned in Mr. Forster's note clearly supports this bird's identification as *decaocto*.—EDS.]

I can remember the secrecy that surrounded the Surrey bird, and those that bred in Norfolk shortly after. The following year, a pair or two nested near my home in Kent (amidst similar secrecy and furtive whispers), but, less than two decades later, numbers in the south-east had increased to such an extent that they were robbing chickens of their food and damaging stored grain! They were subsequently officially classified as a pest. What caused the spread of this Asian species westward across Europe is still a matter of speculation – a sudden genetic mutation (giving the migratory urge) coupled with ecosystems ripe for plunder seems the most likely explanation. Certainly existing British birdlife does not appear to have suffered. The pressures continue:

Continuing immigration of Collared Doves At 15.40 GMT on 5th May 1977, on board a car-ferry 2 km out from Seaford Head and 5 km from Newhaven, off the East Sussex coast and heading northwest, I noticed two Collared Doves *Streptopelia decaocto* approaching from directly astern. They quickly caught up with the ship (which was travelling at 20 knots), briefly checked their speed and flew off strongly northwards, towards Seaford. Robert Hudson (*Brit. Birds* 58: 105-139) showed that this species' dispersal, more or less northwest, occurs mainly between April and June. While it is possible that these two were displaced British birds, the weather was unlikely to have caused such a movement, and continued immigration from the Continent seems probable.

P. F. BONHAM

Now the Collared Dove has swept through Scotland, Ireland and the off-lying Western Islands. I found them on St Kilda, though not breeding, in 1969 and they bred in Iceland not long after. Where next?

Cetti's Warblers were, until the 1960s, considered to be sedentary Mediterranean birds. Atypical warblers, lacking an established migration to escape winter's severity, they began to push north and west and are well documented in this account from Jersey:

Cetti's Warblers in the Channel Islands.—The ringing of three Cetti's Warblers *Cettia cetti* in Jersey, Channel Islands, by members of the Ornithological Section of La Société Jersiaise in 1960, 1961 and 1964 has already been noted in this journal (*Brit. Birds*, 54: 208; 57: 517-518). The retrapping of the third after an interval of three weeks increased speculation about the movements and status of this species in an extensive area of reed-beds and meadows adjoining the bird observatory at St. Ouen's Pond. Now, after a gap of three years, a further series of records has aroused new interest.

The island's fourth Cetti's Warbler was caught and ringed on 22nd October 1967 and then retrapped eight weeks later on 17th December along with a fifth. Yet another, the sixth in all, was trapped on 14th January 1968. Meanwhile, on 26th December a snatch of Cetti's Warbler song was heard and identified by E. D. H. Johnson in company with D. J. Steventon and A. Le Sueur. The last-named was then able to say that some song he had heard on at least two occasions in November had also been that of Cetti's Warbler, and this was subsequently confirmed by Mrs. Le Sueur and my wife when they listened to recordings.

Detailed notes have been taken on each one trapped, but identification in the hand presented no problem after the first in 1960 and the recent ones were recognised immediately, even when seen in a net in fading light. Inspection of the broad, long, first primary then provided the quickest identification. The last to be caught, on 14th January 1968, was brighter and larger (wing 62 mm.) than all the others (wing 55-58 mm.). Its mantle was more rufous, supercilium paler, eye-stripe darker, under-parts whiter and pattern of under tail-coverts more conspicuous. From this we concluded that it was an adult male and that all the others had been females or juveniles.

In view of these several records and the recent extension of the breeding range summarised by I. J. Ferguson-Lees (*Brit. Birds*, 57: 357-359, 518), we now consider that there are likely to be further records and that the species will perhaps even nest. On every occasion that a Cetti's Warbler has been trapped, however, its presence was not suspected beforehand; on release, each one flew immediately to cover and was not seen again. The chances of proving breeding by, say, one or two pairs therefore seem small. R. Long

[In this connection, it is worth noting here that a Cetti's Warbler was trapped at a locality in southern England on 22nd July 1967 and then retrapped on 9th September; at the request of those concerned, locality and names of observers are being suppressed for the time being. All these records are further indication of a northward extension of this species in Europe and it may be only a matter of time before a pair nests here. I have already noted that in 1962 a male was heard singing regularly near Mons, in the Belgian province of Hainaut, and that a nest with five eggs was then discovered there in May 1964 (*Brit. Birds,* 57: 518; and see *Aves,* 1: 49-50). In 1965 one was noted singing in Saint-Denis, also in Hainaut (*Aves,* 4: 60), and further evidence of northward spread in Belgium was provided by the capture of one in the province of West Vlaanderen (*Gerfaut,* 56: 291).—I.J.F.-L.]

Although two birds had been trapped in southern England in 1961 and 1962, it only became apparent in the late 1960s that there were birds resident in southern England. Now, a decade later, and after at least two winters of sufficient severity to test their ability to survive in this country, Cetti's Warblers are not unusual in suitable marshland with damp scrub in the south-eastern corner of England.

The story of the Willow Tit comes from a different age: the tenor of the notes is completely changed, more leisured, and with attention to quite different details. The 'raised eyebrows' of some senior ornithologists of the time at being told that an 'undiscovered' species had been lurking amongst them for many years, are clearly apparent in this note from the first issue of *British Birds*:

REMARKS ON A SUPPOSED NEW BRITISH TIT OF THE GENUS *PARUS*.

BY

P. L. SCLATER, D.SC., F.R.S.

MR. HOWARD SAUNDERS, in his " Manual of British Birds," includes five species of true *Parus* in the British Avifauna, namely, *Parus major*, *P. ater*, *P. palustris*, *P. cœruleus*, and *P. cristatus*.

Dr. Hartert, in his "Vögel der paläarktischen Fauna," in which trinomials are employed, uses for these five species the names *Parus major newtoni*, *P. ater britannicus*, *P. palustris dresseri*, *P. cœruleus obscurus*, and *P. cristatus scoticus*,* on the ground that all the British Tits are subspecifically distinguishable from their continental representatives. But to these five species of *Parus* he adds a sixth, " *Parus atricapillus kleinschmidti*," making it a subspecies of *P. atricapillus* of North America. It is about this form that, as I think, more information is specially required, as its reception as valid would add a new (and very interesting) species to the British List.

The so-called *Parus atricapillus kleinschmidti* seems to have been first indicated by Herr Kleinschmidt in 1898, as a subspecies of *Parus montanus*, though he did not assign any name to it, but simply called it " *Parus montanus* subsp. nov. England " (" Orn. Mon.," vi., p. 34).

In his memoir on the *Paridœ*, published in the " Ornithologisches Jahrbuch for 1900 " (Vol. XI., p. 212), Mr. Hellmayr gave the name *Parus montanus kleinschmidti* to this form, of which he had received for comparison two examples from Dr. Hartert, obtained in the " neighbourhood of London," and now in the Tring Museum. Mr. Hellmayr compares this subspecies with *Parus montanus salicarius* of West and Middle Germany, from which he states that it differs in the darker colouring of the back, which is dark rusty-brown, and in the broad rusty-brown edges of the primaries; the cream-coloured tinge of the sides of the neck extends up to the base of the bill, and surrounds the chin-spot on the front and sides; sides of the neck creamy-yellow; underparts deep rusty-yellow. In the third part of the "Birds of the Palæarctic Fauna," Dr. Hartert, as we have already stated, transfers this subspecies to the group of *Parus atricapillus*, and calls it *Parus atricapillus kleinschmidti* (*op. cit.*, p. 378). He gives its "*terra typica*" as "Coalfall Wood, near Finchley," and states that it is also found near Tunbridge Wells, and in Scotland in the valleys of the Tweed, Forth and Spey.

Some of my friends have suggested that Kleinschmidt's Tit is merely a form of *Parus palustris*. But the British form of *Parus palustris* has been already named *P. palustris dresseri*, and I do not think there can be room for two subspecies of the same species in our little island.

Further explanations concerning *Parus kleinschmidti* and its real status would be very desirable.

° Dr. Hartert writes the subspecific name as *scotica*, but I cannot agree to use false concords. Latin having been universally adopted as the language of science, we are bound, in my opinion, to follow the ordinary rules of its grammar.

Shortly after, some of the differences between the two species were spelt out, but concentration was centred on characteristics observable on the dead specimen in a museum – as was then the general practice.

W. ROTHSCHILD : THE BRITISH WILLOW TIT. 45

The principal differences between the Willow Tits and the Marsh Tits are, *firstly*, that the feathers of the crown and forehead are in the former longer and more loosely constructed, while in the latter they are shorter and more compact. The edges of these feathers in the Marsh Tit are glossy-black, thus causing the whole crown to be glossy and much blacker than that of the Willow Tit, which is of a dull brownish-black or sooty-black; *secondly*, in the Marsh Tits the tail is almost square, while the Willow Tits have it distinctly graduated. Lastly also the notes of the birds are said to be different.

Noticeably absent are comments on the calls and song; on the general shape of the head and neck (the Willow Tit, excavating its own nest hole, is detectably more muscular – bull-necked – in the field); and on the often observable pale fringes to the secondaries which give a distinct 'panel' in the wing. Almost twenty years later, confusion was still evident, though acute observation was generating field characteristics that could be of help.

THE MARSH- AND WILLOW-TIT IN CUMBERLAND.

To the Editors of BRITISH BIRDS.

SIRS,—The only method of establishing the identity of these species is to have specimens examined by some competent authority as Mr. T. L. Johnston has done in the case of the Willow-Tit (*antea*, pp. 96–97) ; identification based solely on breeding-habits is not sufficient, as the following record proves. From 1916 onwards there are various references in my diaries to " black-capped Tits," but to which species they relate I could not say. The heads of these Tits are invariably described as " jet-black " (like the black crown of a male Blackcap) and the alarm-note, when heard, as a " loud and penetrating ' tay-tay-tay.' " In one locality where these Tits exist (and no Woodpeckers have been seen or heard) several drilled holes have been found in dead alder and willow stumps, but no nest found in them.

In this same locality on June 2nd, 1923, a nest of five Tits was found about four inches inside a natural hole in an alder, and the hole showed no signs of having been worked. Both adults were seen, described in my diary as having " jet-black crowns, alarm-note of ' tay-tay-tay.' " After the young had flown the nest was examined and consisted entirely of matted hair-lining. That this case is not exceptional is proved by Mr. Heatley Noble's account (Vol. VII., p. 198) of Tits which, caught on nests in natural holes and drilled holes, were examined by Dr. Hartert and all classified as Marsh-Tits. R. H. BROWN.

[Further evidence with regard to the respective nesting habits of the two species is of course still desirable, but we are unable to accept Mr. Brown's inferences. He proves that the Marsh-Tit nests in his district of Cumberland and his evidence suggests that the Willow-Tit does also. He produces no evidence, however, that the drilled holes were in fact the work of Marsh-Tits. Heatley Noble's evidence, to which Mr. Brown refers, consists of *one* bird obtained from a drilled hole and proved to be a Marsh-Tit, but it was not taken by himself, nor did he see the hole or describe the nest.—EDS.]

THE MARSH- AND WILLOW-TITS IN CUMBERLAND.

To the Editors of BRITISH BIRDS.

SIRS,—Will you allow me to add to the editorial note appended to Mr. R. H. Brown's letter on this subject ? Mr. Brown writes : " The only method of establishing the identity of these species is to have specimens examined by some competent authority." If by this he means only that it is dangerous to state positively that a bird seen in the field, even at quite close quarters, is one or the other, I am inclined to agree with him. Although I generally feel pretty confident of the identity of a silent black-headed Tit seen at close quarters, I am always glad to have the vindication of the distinctive call-notes. These, I can assure Mr. Brown, are absolutely reliable. If he has any difficulty in working out the two sets of call-notes, I would advise him to spend his next holiday in the Alps, and there study the notes and song, first of the black-headed Tit of the high pine-woods (above 1,500 metres) and then of the black-headed Tit of the low deciduous woods (below 1,000 metres). My brother and I first worked out the two sets of notes in England, but subsequently we found our conclusions fully confirmed by experience in countries where the range of the two species does not overlap. I believe a good many British ornithologists are entirely familiar with the two sets of notes.

In recent years I have spent parts of several summers in Cumberland, chiefly near the Solway (Allonby and Maryport district), and also in the Lake District. I have not yet certainly identified a Marsh-Tit, though I rather thought I heard one in the upper part of Borrowdale this summer. The Willow-Tit I have observed several times near Maryport. Comparing Cumberland with most parts of England that I know, however, I should describe both species as scarce. Perhaps I have not visited the wooded districts enough for this opinion to have much value.   H. G. ALEXANDER.

Admittedly, even now we find the separation of Willow Tit from Marsh difficult unless plumage and viewing conditions are good, or unless the bird calls. Certainly, we are still a very long way from explaining the habitat and/or food preferences that separate the two ecologically.

The last section of this chapter is devoted to those species that have come to this country with assisted passages – the deliberate introductions of alien birds. The Mute Swan – perhaps to our surprise as it is now so much a feature of our lives – must have been one of the first:

TWO EARLY RECORDS OF MUTE SWAN IN BEDFORDSHIRE.

THE following is an extract of a Charter, granted to Newnham Priory by William de Beauchamp, taken from *Registrum Cartarum Prioratus de Newenham* (Harl. MS. 3656, f. 8) :—

THE GREAT CHARTER OF WILLIAM DE BEAUCHAMP.
[Undated.]

" To all sons of Holy Mother Church, present and to come : William de Bello Campo, greeting. Know . . . . that I . . . . . have given, granted, and by this present my charter have confirmed, to God and the church of St. Paul of Newenham, any my canons regular serving God there, and to their successors, the church of St. Paul, Bedford . . . .

" Item I have granted to them the whole of Golde(1) mill and the mill which is called of Bedford Castle, together with the new mill, which my father made there, with the places and ponds in which the said mills are built, and with the whole pond from the mills of Bedford Castle, together with the willows and trees growing therein, as far as Joel's pond (*stagnum Joelis*), to plant and to grub up (*assartandum*) and restore (*emendandum*) as often and whensoever they will, freely and quit of all lay service. [f. 8 b.] And I have granted to them that little meadow which lies eastwards of the mills of the Castle, which is called Castelham, and all the water with fishing (*piscacione*) and with all liberties and commodities to the said water pertaining, from the mills of Bedford Castle on the side of (*ex parte*) ' le Sele ' and of the field of Goldyngton ; and all the water from the mill of Joel of Bedford(2), on the side of the meadow of Fenlake, as far as the eastern head of the garden of the said canons and by (*juxta*) the fields of Goldyngton on either side of Swinholm ; and Swinholm itself together with five acres of land which lie by (*iuxta*) Inland from the way of Fenlak, with an island the width of the same land, as far as the pond of the said canons, with all their appurtenances, freely and quietly from all lay service and exaction ; so that no one may have entry [to] that water for fishing without seeking and obtaining their licence. And I have granted to them free entry and re-entry into the said my water with their vessels and boats for carrying whatever they will from the barns of Fenlak to Newenham, and from Newenham to Fenlak, at their will, when necessary. Item I have granted to them for the refreshment of infirm canons, licence to fish twice or three times in the week with nets or with other engines, if they wish, in all my water from the eastern head of their garden as far as the eastern head of the town of Fenlak. And the aforesaid canons shall let rove, swimming and nesting, as many as they wish of their swans, feeding and roving with their hens(3) and cygnets in all my common and several waters throughout the Ouse, from the lordship of the Barony of Eton as far as the lordship of the Barony of Wahull,(4) without challenge or contradiction from me or my heirs, forever. . . ."

Robert Gillmor

Unfortunately, this Charter is undated. The original endowment of the Priory was by Simon de Beauchamp, father of William, who was Baron of Bedford from about A.D. 1165 to A.D. 1206. In the account of the Religious Houses in the *Victorian County History of Bedfordshire*, it reads as though the right of keeping Swans was included in the first or one of the earlier Charters, but no references to Swans are mentioned before this Great Charter of William de Beauchamp, who was Baron from about 1206 to 1260. This Charter can be approximately fixed about A.D. 1210 to A.D. 1225, and I think we can assume that at that time the Mute Swan was of no recent introduction to this country.

In the Records of the alien Priory of Grove, near Leighton Buzzard (*Beds. Hist. Records*, Vol. 8, p. 28), in the sale of stock between Michaelmas 1341-42 are included " 2 Swans sold in the Lady's household," 6s. Comparative values under the same heading occur, cows in winter, 5s. 4d. each, ox 12s., pigs 2s. 6d., Geese and Capons 2½d. each, so Swans seem very high priced by comparison. J. S. ELLIOTT.

(¹) Goldington (J.S.E.).
(²) This may either mean the Bedford mill belonging to one Joel, or the mill belonging to one Joel de Bedford.
(³) Also translated " fledglings " by another transcriber.
(⁴) Odell (J.S.E.).

The editors of *British Birds* articulated the concern felt by many people over the whole topic of 'introductions'.

INTRODUCTION OF BEARDED TITS IN YORKSHIRE.

WE have to record, with great regret, that Mr. W. H. St. Quintin has been at great pains to introduce Bearded Tits (*Panurus biarmicus*) at Hornsea Mere, East Yorkshire. In April, 1911, he liberated six pairs and two odd males, which he had obtained from Holland. Since then these birds have been seen in pairs, and on June 26th a brood was observed, while there may be other broods (*cf. Naturalist*, 1911, pp. 279-80). This passion for interfering with Nature possessed by aviculturists, is likely to do serious harm to the scientific study of ornithology, and is, in its way, almost as bad as the destruction of rare breeding-birds and their eggs by those afflicted with the " British-taken " mania.

In a number of occurrences reported from time to time in our pages, it has been impossible to say if the bird referred to was a genuine migrant or an escape from captivity, and this doubt as to a vagrant being a genuine wild bird or not, increases as more people keep birds in semi-captivity, without even a ring on their legs, or let them loose intentionally. There is the now notorious introduction of the Little Owl, which is increasing to such an extent as to be likely to become very harmful. Attempts to introduce the Willow-Grouse and the American Robin and other birds have, we hope, proved abortive ; but this introduction of Bearded Tits from the Continent is nearly as bad as the attempt to introduce Willow-Grouse ; and it can only be hoped that Mr. St. Quintin's aliens will be banished in some way or other.

As the Dutch birds are migratory and not sedentary like ours, we trust these imported birds will follow their hereditary instincts, and that they will not return.   THE EDITORS.

Perhaps in the case of the 'Scilly budgies' there is little real cause for alarm.

Free-winged Budgerigars in the Isles of Scilly   Dr J. T. R. Sharrock

(1976, *The Atlas of Breeding Birds in Britain and Ireland*, page 452) summarised the status of feral Budgerigars *Melopsittacus undulatus* in England. For several years, I have observed those on Tresco, Isles of Scilly, and their history seems worth recording. In 1969, four pairs were introduced to Tresco from Windsor Lodge, Berkshire; in autumn 1970, six more pairs were added (Mrs P. Dorrien Smith *in litt.*). These and some of their progeny bred in all 16 nestboxes in an aviary in the abbey gardens. In 1972, however, the aviary was permanently open and they bred away from it, although visiting it daily for food or for roosting in poor weather; many also fed on food thrown to tame geese (Anatidae) in the meadows, from nearby chicken pens, or on seeds of wild plants. At first, these Budgerigars nested in holes in cordylines *Cordyline* and palms (Palmaceae); later, they occupied holes in elms *Ulmus*, sycamores *Acer pseudoplatanus* and other tall trees, all, I believe, in the vicinity of the abbey gardens. Because of the amount of foliage, I could not ascertain whether they excavated the holes or enlarged existing ones. By 1974, about 35 nests were in use, with 30 or more non-breeding Budgerigars in the area. During the summer, they separated into two main, discrete flocks which came together very late in the afternoon and stayed in and near the breeding trees in the wood, where they no doubt roosted. One flock, of 20 to 30 individuals, consorted with Starlings *Sturnus vulgaris* in the fields, but neither the latter nor the ubiquitous House Sparrows *Passer domesticus* showed any aggression towards the Budgerigars. Whenever the Starlings took flight and flew around at heights, the Budgerigars would accompany them, both species calling loudly. They would take brief refuge in the bushes and then return slowly in small groups to the seed fields.

I sent a few specimens of the Budgerigars' food plants to the keeper of botany at the British Museum (Natural History), who identified the following: annual meadow-grass *Poa annua*, toad rush *Juncus bufonius*, slender sandwort *Arenaria leptoclados*, pearlwort *Sagina* (possibly annual pearlwort *S. apetala*) and swine-cress *Coronopus*. I also observed some Budgerigars perching on the side of the abbey wall and methodically pecking out pieces of the prostrate leaves of navelwort *Umbilicus rupestris*. J. E. Lousley (1971, *The Flora of the Isles of Scilly*, page 181) mentioned that this grows where salt concentration is high; perhaps the Budgerigars were obtaining certain beneficial mineral residues. On occasions, groups picked up grit from the ground.

Mrs Dorrien Smith, who had provided artificial food for the birds, left the island in 1974, after which regular food may not have been put out. During April 1975, I found the population greatly depleted, and during ten days in October that year failed to see a single Budgerigar on Tresco.

BERNARD KING
Gull Cry, 9 Park Road, Newlyn, Penzance, Cornwall

The Ring-necked Parakeet has generated a very different reaction:

Feral populations of parrakeets Most readers will already be aware that the Ringneck Parrakeet* *Psittacula krameri* has succeeded in establishing a feral population in several parts of England, for example Essex, Kent (two areas) and Surrey (two widely separated areas) (*Brit. Birds*, 67: 33, 174). Although escapes may have added to their number, deliberate liberation has almost certainly been the main cause.

In my opinion some other species of parrots are equally capable and the reason for the success of the Ringneck is probably its cheapness, not its greater capacity to survive English winters. Admittedly we have not recently had a winter harsh enough to put it to a severe test, but its almost omnivorous readiness to take advantage of food put out for other birds would undoubtedly ensure its survival except in quite abnormally prolonged hard weather. The practice of keeping free-flying birds for the pleasure of seeing them around appears to be growing in favour and the Ringneck, since it is imported in great numbers and is cheaper than most other similar species, has had a flying start in establishing itself. No one would deny that a flock of parrots flying round the garden is most attractive; no serious ornithologists would deny the dangers of such liberations.

At present the number of feral Ringnecks is comparatively small; at this stage it would not be difficult to stop the nonsense (to put it at its lowest) of a parrot getting on the British and Irish list, by trapping and incarcerating them; before long it may be too late. Our grandchildren will not thank us for a bird which could so easily become a menace to fruit and other crops, quite apart from its success in taking over nest-holes needed by other species and generally becoming an ecological nuisance.

Those who have access to American literature will have seen that a similar, if not worse, state of affairs is giving cause for alarm over there. Areas as far apart as south-east Florida, the environs of New York City and southern California all have increasing problems with introduced or escaped birds, especially parrots, which have established themselves in a feral state, in some cases now beyond the reasonable possibility of control (*Wilson Bull.*, 85: 491-512).

Many reasons have been advanced for the urgent need to re-instate the 'Parrot Ban' (a former restriction on the importation into Britain of parrots, rather similar to that currently applying to birds of prey), among them the obvious conservational one and the very real danger of ornithosis to human health. A not-to-be-despised addition to these reasons is the need to prevent Britain from being overrun by a potential pest, however attractive this pest may appear to be.   M. D. ENGLAND

Feral parrakeets and control of introductions M. D. England's concern (*Brit. Birds*, 67: 393-394) over feral populations of the Ringneck Parrakeet *Psittacula krameri* may be heightened by my experience of this species. I first saw one at liberty in Wallington, Surrey, on 18th September 1962 and thereafter saw it almost daily throughout the abnormally prolonged hard weather of the winter that followed, my last sighting being on 16th March 1963. I understand it was then 'recaptured' by its alleged owner. Thus, with access to food especially put out, it demonstrated its ability to survive until some ten days after the last traces of snow had vanished. During the most severe weather it roosted nightly in a group of trees, predominantly elm, in a nearby recreation ground.
                                                              K. D. G. MITCHELL

In a recent letter in which he advocated the elimination of feral populations of parrakeets now living in southern England, M. D. England referred to the situation in parts of the USA where several introduced bird species have become pests. There are, of course, notable examples in Britain of introductions producing serious pests. One such species is the Grey Squirrel *Sciurus carolinensis*, introduced in the 1890's and already a major pest in broadleaved woodland in England, Wales and parts of southern Scotland. The Forestry Commission rates this species as a greater threat, through its bark-stripping activities, to our broadleaved trees than that facing our elms from the aggressive strain of Dutch Elm Disease. It is also a predator on the nestlings of some of our native birds. All that can be done now is to undertake such control measures as limit the damage to broadleaved trees to an acceptable level.

The lesson from this and other examples—such as the Coypu *Myocastor coypus* and Mink *Mustela vison*—is quite clear. Introductions should be made, or captive species liberated, only after a thorough examination of the probable consequences, and subsequent developments properly monitored. Uncontrolled populations should be eliminated before they become so widespread that such action is no longer possible. In the present instance, the added risk to human health from ornithosis makes this a clear case for immediate action.
                                                              R. B. TOZER

A full-scale enquiry, to determine their present status, has been set up because of mounting concern amongst fruit-growers (and, to be fair, amongst many naturalists) at the potential impact of such a successful bird.

Ring-necked Parakeets   The main concentrations of the Ring-necked Parakeet *Psittacula krameri* in Britain are in southeast England, but there is now evidence of breeding elsewhere. Numbers have increased steadily for the last ten years, and in the last two the population in Kent has doubled to 100-200 pairs, with winter flocks of up to 45 on the Isle of Thanet and 69 near Bromley.

The species has been imported in considerable numbers from Asia (and a few from Africa) in recent years; it is the commonest imported parakeet and also the cheapest, with prices as low as £8.00. Some escape; others are deliberately released either because people find that they do not make good pets or to produce attractive free-flying flocks.

So far in Britain, Ring-necked Parakeets are concentrated mainly in the vicinity of human habitations, such as town parks and gardens, but also occur in farmland. There is no evidence that hard winters reduce their numbers, since, in the urban areas where most of them live, they have a choice of ample food put out by bird-lovers. They frequently visit garden bird-tables and nut feeders, usually in the early morning and late afternoon (plate 134). They rarely take food from the ground.

In Britain, the breeding season is from February to June. The nest-site is normally high in a hollow tree or in a hole excavated by another bird, but they also enlarge existing holes with great gusto; they not infrequently take over nest-sites that would otherwise be used by native species later in the year.

Damage in Kent has included eating tree buds and garden rose buds in spring, tearing flowers to pieces in summer and feeding on apples on the trees in autumn (their most frequent destructive habit). The time may come when it is necessary to classify them officially as pests. There are probably about 1,000 living ferally in at least 16 counties in England and Scotland; it is doubtful whether it would now be possible to exterminate them here. In the USA, similar problems have arisen with feral Monk Parakeets *Mycopsitta monachus*, which are proving difficult to eradicate.

An enquiry into the past and present status of the Ring-necked Parakeet in southeast England, including the numbers and damage done to garden and farm crops, is now being launched, with the support of the BTO and co-operation of D. J. Montier (6 Cloonmore Avenue, Orpington, Kent) who is collecting London area records. Please send details of autumn and winter flocks, breeding records (including numbers of young reared and species of tree used), information about feeding from bird-tables and damage done in gardens, parks and agricultural areas to Brian Hawkes, 55 The Street, Newnham, Sittingbourne, Kent ME9 0LN.

⤙ 7 ⤚

Aggression

Aggression between different species of birds, between individuals of the same species, and between birds and other animals (including man) that are, or may be, predators, takes a variety of forms. At one level, it is just an aspect of the interaction between predator and prey, as this detailed account of the trials and tribulations of being a Puffin shows.

Techniques of Herring Gulls and Jackdaws preying on Puffins.— While making a film of sea-birds in Pembrokeshire in the summer of 1959, I spent many hours on the island of Skomer watching the Puffins (*Fratercula arctica*). I became especially interested in their behaviour in relation to that of their two chief enemies at the time of feeding their young (mid-June to August), namely the Herring Gulls (*Larus argentatus*) and the Jackdaws (*Corvus monedula*). Both these species would wait on the cliff-tops above the colonies, individual birds seeming to occupy regular "beats". From such vantage points they would pounce on any returning Puffin in order to rob it of its beakful of fish as it ran to its burrow mouth. As a result, the Puffins became extremely wary and nervous, often flying round in a wide circle a dozen times before choosing the moment to land and then disappearing down the burrow with remarkable agility.

The Herring Gulls (on both Skomer and the neighbouring island of Skokholm) used several different techniques to catch the Puffins during the vital seconds between their landing and their disappearance down the burrow. Some attempts to chase birds in flight were observed, but these were very seldom successful, the Puffin nearly always escaping with a rapid dive towards the sea. On a few occasions, however, a Herring Gull was seen to continue the pursuit down to the water, whereupon the Puffin would drop its food and this would then be immediately picked from the surface by its tormentor. Once a Puffin let go its fish at its burrow mouth when first attacked and yet was still pursued by the marauder for several hundred yards out to sea; but the gull may have been unaware that the food had been dropped. Certainly on no occasion was a Herring Gull seen to attack an adult Puffin itself, and the only one observed to kill a fully fledged young Puffin took half an hour to do so and was then quite unable to eat it on the water. Great Black-backed Gulls (*L. marinus*), by contrast, could disembowel Puffins in a matter of seconds after killing them.

Some Herring Gulls remained on the wing and quartered the colony while watching for the arrival of Puffins carrying food. Such birds were not nearly so successful, however, as those which stood near the burrows (or even some distance away) and pounced only as Puffins came in to land. Presumably this was because the ones which remained on the ground were not so conspicuous and one in particular brought this to a fine art.

This gull had its beat just in front of my photographic hide on a cliff-top in the middle of a large Puffin colony. It paid very little attention to humans, virtually ignoring me as I entered the hide and perching on top even when I was inside. At first it just waited, as the others did, watching the endless procession of Puffins flying past. Whenever one which was carrying food approached, its eyes would intently follow that bird's flight, so much so that one could tell what was happening by watching the gull. The grass where it waited was mostly longish and I noted that it began deliberately to crouch in the cover this afforded whenever a food-carrying Puffin started to fly in. After a few days it evolved a clear-cut and regular technique of "hiding" in the grass, with only its head showing, until the Puffin had actually landed. Once the habit had been formed, this gull would flex its legs and squat down on the approach of a Puffin even when it was standing in the open, though this then had little effect in rendering it inconspicuous.

Study of the several film sequences obtained of this Herring Gull confirm the field observations. If the Puffin landed near-by, the gull would attack at once; if further away, it would often wait in a very tense attitude for a considerable time before the wary (and usually clearly terrified) Puffin would dare to approach and make a dash for its burrow. It was most interesting to watch the battle of wits which thus followed when a Puffin landed just too far away to stimulate an immediate attack from the gull, and it provided the strongest impression of birds "thinking" I have ever witnessed. Both gull and Puffin, perhaps only ten yards apart, would stand watching each other intently, each providing a stimulus to the other but in neither case strongly enough to produce a reaction. The mental struggle for the Puffin between fleeing and feeding its chick was usually resolved in favour of approaching the burrow, provided that the gull remained still. For the gull it appeared to be a more subtle conflict between attacking at too great a distance and waiting for its victim to move, either reaction (when considered in human terms) seeming to involve an element of calculated risk. During this waiting period, indeed from the moment the Puffin landed, the gull almost invariably stood up: this was as clear a reaction as its crouching when the other first approached. The "hiding" technique was most successful against Puffins which landed near-by, but it is hard to say whether it was more successful than the normal method of waiting out in the open. Certainly, however, it earned this particular Herring Gull many a meal of sand-eels designed for nestlings underground (though on at least one occasion it achieved only a beakful of feathers).

As mentioned at the beginning, the Jackdaws also attacked the food-carrying Puffins. Like the Herring Gulls, they would wait along the cliff edge and pursue them both in flight and as they ran to their burrows, though (again like the gulls) they would sit amongst a crowd of empty-billed Puffins at the cliff-top without molesting them. The Jackdaws were frequently seen to eat the fish dropped, probably mostly whitebait and sand-eels, though fish are not mentioned in *The Handbook* as a food of this species. Later in the season they were also observed carrying fish in their crops to their nests or feeding them direct to fully-fledged young on the spot. Fish, in fact, play a large part in the diet of the Jackdaw on Skomer, probably a result of the huge increase in the population of this species there in recent years: in 1946 about twenty pairs were estimated, but now it would clearly be no exaggeration to say that hundreds of pairs breed all round the island. In this connection, I also recorded Jackdaws eating Herring Gulls' eggs and the refuse round the nest of a pair of Great Black-backed Gulls, and there was a continual procession of them flying to and from the mainland for food. C. K. MYLNE

SLAUGHTER OF MANX SHEARWATERS BY BLACK-BACKED GULLS.

ON the island of Annet in the Scilly Islands, large numbers of sea-birds breed, consisting chiefly of Greater and Lesser Black-backed Gulls, Puffins, Manx Shearwaters, Herring-Gulls, Razorbills, and a few Oyster-catchers and some Shags. Large numbers of Manx Shearwaters (*Puffinus anglorum*) are slain by the two species of Black-backed Gulls, their skins, in many cases turned inside out, being found in scores on the ground frequented by these two species. Puffins are also treated in a similar manner, but many fewer of these birds are killed. All the remains I saw were dried up, but Mr. C. J. King, of St. Mary's, informs me that he has often found them freshly killed, and that they are done to death by the Gulls tearing a hole in the abdomen to devour the entrails—literally, I take it, drawing the unfortunate birds when living. The Razorbills are evidently too formidable for even the Greater Black-backed Gull to tackle, as they are left very much alone, and I do not wonder at it, judging by the adults which I handled, the thickest leather gauntlets being no protection whatsoever against their formidable beaks. The Puffins do not seem to have any fear of the Lesser Black-backed Gull, judging by the way they sit cheek by jowl on the same rock, so perhaps it is only the larger species which disembowels them. Owing to my visiting the island by day, I only saw one living Manx Shearwater, this being one which I picked up in a landing-net at sea, about two miles from the island in question, but the number nesting there is estimated locally at between a hundred and a hundred-and-fifty thousand.

H. W. ROBINSON.

[In a most interesting article on the Puffin by Mr. F. Heatherley, which appeared in *Country Life*, September 3rd, 1910, it is stated that colonies of the Lesser Black-backed Gull are always strewn with corpses of Puffins, which have been merely disembowelled and left. On the other hand the colonies of the Greater Black-backed Gulls contain no corpses, possibly because they have been swallowed by the larger birds ! Mr. Heatherley has never actually seen this take place, but he quotes the evidence of Mr. J. W. Parsons, who states that before being swallowed the Puffin is shaken and ducked under water until drowned. The capacity of the larger Gulls for swallowing is certainly remarkable, and only a week or two ago I saw a Mediterranean Herring-Gull pick up a good-sized vole from the water in which it was swimming, and gulp it down alive.—F. C. R. JOURDAIN.

The "skinning" of the Manx Shearwaters, described by Mr. Robinson, is much more likely to have been the work of rats than Gulls, although the rats may have finished the carcases and left the skins after the Gulls had partially eaten them.—EDS.]

The gory destruction wrought by some Great Black-back Gulls now seems well known, but it is interesting to see from the editorial footnote that, in 1912, the skilful abilities of this gull at skinning other unfortunate sea-birds had not been fully recognised.

Sometimes, however, the aggression comes from unexpected quarters: few would have supposed the elusive, even retiring, Water Rail capable of such deeds:

Water Rail drowning small Passerines.—At about 1.0 p.m. on 4th January 1962, when there were four inches of snow on the ground but it was not actually snowing, my wife called me to look out of the window of our cottage at Cavenham Mill, near Bury St. Edmunds, Suffolk, at the way a Water Rail (*Rallus aquaticus*) was behaving. A few moments before I had cast out half a pint of crushed oats and crumbs and the Water Rail was making threatening rushes at the House Sparrows (*Passer domesticus*), Great Tits (*Parus major*), Blue Tits (*P. caeruleus*) and other birds which were feeding there. I thought at first that it was just trying to scare them away so that it could have the food to itself, but suddenly it seized what I think was a Dunnock (*Prunella modularis*) in its beak and carried it swiftly down to the edge of the mill-pool some twenty feet from our front door. There the Water Rail stepped into shallow water and held its captive right under until it was dead, whereupon it started to peck at it.

Later the same day, at about 3.0 p.m., I happened to glance out of the window again and saw the Water Rail drowning another bird. This time it seemed to be a hen Chaffinch (*Fringilla coelebs*). The Water Rail was also seen to pick to bits a dead Song Thrush (*Turdus philomelos*) which had been killed by the frost and which we had thrown down on the edge of the pool.   ALFRED R. BLUNDELL

Water Rail killing and eating small passerines.—On 7th January 1968, at West Rudham, Norfolk, I saw a Water Rail *Rallus aquaticus* feeding on seeds which I had put out for finches on the ground round the base of my bird table. It would pick up and swallow a few seeds and then take two or three draughts of water from a pan provided for the birds. It appeared to be in poor condition with dull, fluffed out plumage. During the next few days the weather deteriorated and much snow fell, whereupon the Water Rail started to attack the smaller birds feeding round the bird table. It would remain perfectly still in the cover of some Brussels sprouts and, as soon as a bird came near enough, it would dart out and attempt to seize it, often displacing bunches of feathers when it failed to secure a hold. When it did succeed in grasping one firmly in its bill, it would beat it to death on the frozen ground or on the legs of the bird table, like a Song Thrush *Turdus philomelos* breaking open snails. Having killed its victim, it would take it to a particular place under a rose bush near-by and start to pluck it; after removing a few patches of feathers from the under-side, it would begin to eat the flesh of the breast, quickly tearing it away from the neck to the vent. Once it had left a carcase partly eaten I never saw it return to finish it off.

In all I saw the Water Rail kill and eat in this way nine individuals of five species—two Dunnocks *Prunella modularis*, two Greenfinches *Carduelis chloris*, two Chaffinches *Fringilla coelebs*, one House Sparrow *Passer domesticus* and two Tree Sparrows *P. montanus*. As it used to come at the same time each morning, I probably witnessed most of the occasions on which it was successful. Once, however, it struck at a bird at dusk: the intended victim flew through the rose bush and the Water Rail went after it like a hawk, but became tangled in the branches. When it left the garden on 16th January, it was in sleek, compact plumage and prime condition. I have lived and worked in the country all my life, but have never before seen this side of the Water Rail's character.   A. V. HOLLIDAY

[In 1962 we printed several notes on Water Rails beating to death or drowning small birds (*Brit. Birds*, 55: 132-133, 165 and 275). The species concerned were Wren *Troglodytes troglodytes*, Dunnock, Chaffinch and Little Stint *Calidris minuta* and other references were made to published records involving Twite *Acanthis flavirostris* and Greenfinch. It was concluded that such predatory activities by Water Rails were probably much less uncommon than had been supposed. Nevertheless, Mr. Holliday's record is unusually detailed and of particular interest since it concerns regular observations over several days.—EDS.]

Obviously, on occasion, unknown forces can drive birds that we regard as placid inhabitants of our gardens into horrific acts of violence. We are familiar with bullying at the bird-table, or occasional skirmishes – mostly bluster – between neighbouring male Blackbirds, but not this:

Great Tit killing and carrying Goldcrest.—On 20th January 1958, Mr. W. French and I were walking near the River Irthing just above Lanercost, near Brampton, Cumberland. It was a very bitter day. As we followed a low drystone wall on the edge of a wood, a Great Tit (*Parus major*) fluttered along the ground and flew up into an elderberry bush some 5-6 feet high. Something appeared to be attached to the bird's feet and at first we thought it was some foreign material entangled in the claws. When we approached, the tit flew very heavily into the next bush, after which it was flushed in turn from quite a number of bushes and sometimes flew distances of 12-15 yards. Eventually it tired and settled on the ground inside the wood, whereupon it started to peck at the object it had been carrying with it. We watched the

scene for a few minutes; then my companion crept up against the wall and succeeded in frightening the bird so that it dropped the object—which we had by then concluded must be a mouse. Imagine our surprise on picking up a Goldcrest (*Regulus regulus*), which was still warm. It had been killed by a peck at the back of the skull, the eyes had been eaten and the head was badly torn. What particularly amazed us both, however, was the manner in which the tit carried the Goldcrest in its feet, as would a hawk.

J. L. CARIS

[We showed this remarkable observation to Dr. David Lack, but he was unable to produce any parallel from the studies of Great Tits carried out by the Edward Grey Institute, Oxford. The second observer has sent us an independent letter of confirmation, and the careful and detailed description seems to exclude any possibility of an error. Great Tits have keen known to kill "a bat and young birds, attacking the brain" (*The Handbook*, vol. I, p. 248) and will sometimes also attack other birds caught with them in cage-traps.—EDS.]

Great Tit probably killing Blue Tit at the nest   On 11th May 1974 a nest box in a wood near Brecon, Powys, was found to contain the presumed egg of a Blue Tit *Parus caeruleus*. On 15th May the box was empty but on 18th May another egg was seen and there was a dead Blue Tit, its skull crushed, depressed into the side of the nest. Five days later a Great Tit *P. major* was sitting and hissed and darted aggressively as I peered in. This bird eventually reared six young which were ready to fly on 23rd June. When the nest was removed it was found to be covering three eggs of Blue Tit size and one of Great Tit size, all undeveloped.

It is possible that the Great Tit took the nest over after the Blue Tit had been killed by a predator but it is unlikely that a predator would have left three eggs and a corpse unconsumed. A more probable explanation is that the Great Tit attacked and killed the Blue Tit on 13th or 14th May, when the latter would have had at least three eggs. The dead bird and the eggs would then have been pushed to one side for the intruder to proceed with her own laying. Though a certain amount of competition between the two species seems to be common, I have seen no reference to its going this far.   DUNCAN J. BROWN

16 Dorlangoch, Brecon, Powys

Robin killing nestling Song Thrushes   In April 1977, in AB's garden at Higher Bebington, Merseyside, a pair of Song Thrushes *Turdus philomelos* nested in a hedge of hawthorn *Crataegus monogyna*, and a pair of Robins *Erithacus rubecula* built in a nestbox about 15 m away. The thrush laid its eggs about ten days before the Robin. Soon after the Robin had laid, there were a number of conflicts with the adult thrushes, usually close to the latter's nest. When the Robin's eggs hatched, on about 5th May, a Robin made a series of raids on the thrushes' nest and, despite the frantic activity of the adults, succeeded in killing three of the four nestlings, by severely pecking at their skulls. The surviving youngster escaped along the hedgerow, but its parents had to defend it vigorously against the Robin. Neither the adult nor fledgling Song Thrush was seen in the garden again. Although Robins are renowned for territorial conflict, we know of no incident similar to that described.   P. COFFEY and A. BOYD

116 Ennisdale Drive, West Kirby, Wirral, Merseyside L48 9HB

These events are in marked contrast to those recorded previously (*Brit. Birds* 61: 34), involving a Robin feeding nestling thrushes. EDS

Dunnock killing Dunnock   Dr Bruce Campbell's note (*Brit. Birds*, 67: 121-122) on one Robin *Erithacus rubecula* killing another reminded us of an incident witnessed by half a dozen members of the staff of the Royal Society for the Protection of Birds at The Lodge, Sandy, Bedfordshire, on 4th March 1970.

Snow had been falling all day, eventually lying to a depth of up to 30 cm, and the bird tables were well patronised. Casual observations at one of these, overlooked by a window in The Lodge, included a number of sightings of a particularly aggressive Dunnock *Prunella modularis* vigorously and continuously chasing another, with occasional brief flurries of actual fighting. Finally, somebody noticed that one of these, no doubt the aggressive bird, was standing on the prostrate but still living body of another small bird; as we watched, the former was seen plucking out the latter's crown feathers literally by the beakful, between delivering numerous heavy blows with its bill. The depth and softness of the snow made it difficult to see precisely what had happened to the victim. After a few minutes MJE went out to look and found the corpse of a Dunnock, its crown stripped bare of feathers and beaten to a bloody pulp. Subsequent examination revealed that the cranium had been cracked in at least two places.

The persistence of the aggressor was surprising in itself, but the savagery of what appeared to have been a brief struggle and the damage to the victim's skull were quite remarkable.

MICHAEL J. EVERETT and NICHOLAS HAMMOND
RSPB, The Lodge, Sandy, Bedfordshire SG19 2DL

Dr K. E. L. Simmons informs us that in spring 1974 he and his wife watched a prolonged fight between two Dunnocks which were spreadeagled and interlocked—claws-to-claws, breast-to-breast—for at least ten minutes. EDS

Starling interfering with Blackbird's nest Geoff Shaw's note (*Brit. Birds* 70: 394) on the apparent predation of the eggs of a Robin *Erithacus rubecula* by a Blue Tit *Parus caeruleus* prompts me to record the following. In 1975, a pair of Blackbirds *Turdus merula* nested in a cherry laurel *Prunus laurocerasus* 10 m from the window of my house in York. On 4th June, the nest held four young about five days old. At 10.10 GMT I was attracted by the persistent, agitated alarm calls of the female, sitting on a hedge next to the laurel. After a few minutes, she flew into the bush, 'pinking' loudly, and what was obviously a fight ensued inside the bush; she then emerged together with a Starling *Sturnus vulgaris*. The Blackbird immediately returned to the bush, presumably to brood her young; the Starling flew away, but within minutes returned and re-entered the bush. Both birds were invisible to me, but there was considerable movement around the nest, with 'pinking' by the Blackbird and periods of subdued singing by the Starling; from time to time, one or both burst out into the open. This lasted for nearly 45 minutes, until I decided to look at the nest. When I approached, the Starling flew 30 m to a tree on which there was a nestbox containing a Starling's nest; the Blackbird flew away. The Blackbird's nest was considerably disturbed with grass scattered from the rim; two of the young were bleeding profusely from the head and back, while the other two appeared unharmed.

Within minutes of my returning to the house, the Starling reappeared, and for a time sang loudly from inside the bush near the nest. At 11.10 hours, the Blackbird returned, and fighting broke out again. I formed the impression that the Starling was trying to stay very close to, if not actually on, the nest, and that the Blackbird was trying to eject it. I had to leave the house at 11.15, with the fight still going on; when I returned at 15.00, the nest was badly damaged and empty, and there was no sign of Starling, Blackbird or young.

At no stage did I see the male Blackbird. The most remarkable thing was the frenzied persistence of the Starling in trying to get on, or very near to, the Blackbird's nest, which was visible from above through a hole in the canopy of the bush; and the viciousness of the fights. I suspect that the Starling was nesting in the box 30 m away. The behaviour might be explained as misdirected parental care by the Starling, which was trying to brood the young Blackbirds (these presumably being accidentally injured in the ensuing fight). Predation seems unlikely since the Starling sang, at times very loudly, from inside the bush.

J. H. LAWTON

Department of Biology, University of York, Heslington, York YO1 5DD

The interpretation of these strange events is difficult; we hope, therefore, that any comparable observations will be reported to us. EDS

The defence of territory, nest or young, against intruders is more expected.

UNUSUAL BOLDNESS OF ROBIN IN DEFENCE OF YOUNG.

BIRDS in London gardens are no doubt frequently influenced in their behaviour by constant proximity to human beings, so that this may account for the unusual boldness of a Robin (*Erithacus r. melophilus*) in my garden at Hampstead. This bird has a nest containing young in some ivy on a fence about five feet from the ground. When sitting the bird was remarkably tame and allowed people to crowd round and look at it without moving from the nest. But since the young have hatched the bird swoops down at everyone who approaches the nest closely. If one puts one's head or one's hand close to the nest it darts down, brushing it with its wings and hitting it with its feet and occasionally with its beak as well. Usually it does not strike very hard, but once it just drew blood. The swoop is made from a branch three or four feet above the nest, and the descent is at an angle of about 45°. After striking, the bird sometimes continues its descent to the ground and sometimes rises to another bough overhead. Its persistence in this performance is remarkable, and so long as one keeps quite close to the nest it continues to swoop, making each time the little hissing " tick " which signifies anger.

Yet the bird will feed the young without hesitation when several people are standing within a few feet of the nest, and attacks only when a nearer approach is made. Whether it is the cock or the hen I cannot say, but for the last few days only one bird has fed the young or appeared, though during incubation the male was constantly feeding the female on the nest.   H. F. WITHERBY.

Shelducks diving at a Marsh Harrier in unison.—On 15th June 1959, in Suffolk, I witnessed an attack by a pair of Shelducks (*Tadorna tadorna*) on a Marsh Harrier; it seemed remarkable both for its duration and the method employed. A pair of Marsh Harriers were breeding in an extensive reed-bed and for fully an hour and a quarter the male was flying continuously to and fro over the area, often at a height of about a hundred feet. For almost the whole of this time it was being harassed by the Shelducks, both of which flew after it and now and then at it. Towards the end of the period I watched them, however, a different method was used. The Shelducks, flying close together, climbed well above the harrier which was itself at a fairly considerable height. They then turned and dived at it in unison. Their previous attacks had been avoided without apparent effort, but this time the harrier was forced to side-slip and drop many feet in the process. Such an action on the part of the Shelducks, which presumably had young in the vicinity, would seem to be very unusual and I have been unable to trace a similar occurrence.   C. M. VEYSEY

Nevertheless, pressing home the attack to its conclusion is a rarely recorded event.

Carrion Crows killing Kestrel.—On 27th July 1962, at Hilfield Park Reservoir, Hertfordshire, I watched three Carrion Crows (*Corvus corone*)—two adults and a juvenile—attack a female Kestrel (*Falco tinnunculus*). The adult crows had a nest and the falcon happened to settle in the same line of trees. The episode took place in the top of a tree and it was very difficult to see anything because of the leaves, but the fact remains that the Kestrel shortly fell to the ground and died within a few seconds, apparently of a broken neck.

On 2nd September 1962, at the same locality, I watched a solitary Carrion Crow make repeated attacks on a female Kestrel in flight. The chase continued over the reservoir and through surrounding trees for about ten minutes, during which time two more crows joined the original attacker. On several occasions the Kestrel was forced almost to the ground, but eventually she escaped by superior flight and manoeuvrability.   BRYAN L. SAGE

Sometimes, it may *seem* that there has been a mistake, as Dr Sharrock records.

Birds mobbing Collared Dove   On several occasions in April, May and June 1977, at Blunham, Bedfordshire, the cause of a commotion among the resident Blackbirds *Turdus merula*, Song Thrushes *T. philomelos*, Greenfinches *Carduelis chloris* and Chaffinches *Fringilla coelebs* in a 3½-m hedge of yew *Taxus baccata* was not the expected domestic cat *Felis* or Tawny Owl *Strix aluco*, but a Collared Dove *Streptopelia decaocto*. When surrounded by the noisy, mobbing group, the dove hung precariously on the side of the hedge in a near-vertical position, with wings and tail spread, in a submissive, apparently cowering or cringing attitude; on each occasion, it flew off unpursued after two or three minutes and the mobbing birds immediately became silent. The first time that I investigated, I expected to find a predator and, seeing a medium-sized pale grey bird being mobbed, called to my family to come and see the Cuckoo *Cuculus canorus*, although I realised my error almost at once. I assume that the mobbing birds were making the same mistake.

J. T. R. SHARROCK
Fountains, Park Lane, Blunham, Bedford MK44 3NJ

Birds in general have a fairly large repertoire of techniques for dealing with predators. Dr Bourne debates the functions of 'mobbing'; Mr Hudson instances their inherent alertness.

Rotating of resting Curlew.—At about 9 a.m. on 6th February 1964, near Rochester, Kent, I watched two Curlew *Numenius arquata* resting on a marsh some 50 yards away. Each was standing on one leg, one with its head hunched on its shoulders and the other with its bill tucked into its scapulars. The former was continually moving its head from side to side through an angle of 30-40°, but the latter was rotating its whole body through 45-50° about the axis of the leg on which it was standing—each rotation, one way or the other, being accomplished by two or three slightly jerky movements.

I was unable to see the left side of this bird's head, but it certainly had its right eye open. Resting waders are always on the look-out for potential danger and constant movements of the head are necessary to increase the range of vision. However, when one has its bill buried in its scapulars, head movements are impossible and it seemed to me that this particular Curlew was solving the problem by rotating its whole body. In spite of the obvious survival value of such behaviour, I have not previously observed anything of the kind or been able to find a published reference to it.   M. J. HUDSON

[It is not unusual for dozing waders, gulls and ducks to turn or 'sway' from side to side and we believe that Mr. Hudson's interpretation is probably correct, though we have not seen it suggested before.—EDS.]

The function of mobbing Mobbing is a well-known phenomenon in which a number of birds, often of different species, unite to make an outcry when they detect a predator, or some other strange or sick bird; the behaviour tends to be most conspicuous when young birds leave the nest. Two obvious functions are to warn potential victims to lie low, while at the same time distracting the predator. The occurrence of mobbing has been widely used in ethological studies as a test of predator-recognition (Curio 1963, Galloway 1972), without much consideration of its function. Simmons (1952) has suggested that it arises as a result of a conflict between tendencies to attack and flee, Hinde (1954) that curiosity may also be involved, Marler (1956) that it may help indicate areas to avoid, and Kruuk (1976) that it is a means of communicating past bad experience. There appears to be a deficiency of accounts of the outcome of natural incidents, and at least one additional function is not mentioned in a review of animal defence mechanisms by Edmunds (1974). It may therefore be useful to describe what happens in nature.

During the fine, sunny afternoon of 29th June 1975, I was walking through a natural wood of Scots pines *Pinus sylvestris* in Glentanar, Grampian, when my attention was attracted by a distant clamour from at least six Chaffinches *Fringilla coelebs*, and a pair each of Willow Warblers *Phylloscopus trochilus*, Coal Tits *Parus ater* and Treecreepers *Certhia familiaris*. Closer inspection revealed that the birds were hopping about agitatedly and approaching within 30 cm of the tail of an adder *Vipera berus* projecting from behind the piece of dead bark covering the Treecreepers' nest, 1 m above the ground on the bole of a pine tree. The snake had already swallowed one fledgling and killed two more when I intervened

and allowed at least one more to escape. The birds took no notice of me until then, when they all departed, except the Treecreepers, which continued to express anxiety less obtrusively. I would never have found the snake if the birds had not directed my attention to it, and I doubt if they could have got rid of it in any other way. Doubtless any other predator, such as a bird of prey, would have been similarly attracted.

The function of the classical hue and cry was to embarrass a human malefactor and secure his apprehension by the first person strong enough. In the present case, it seemed unnecessary to warn other birds to lie low, and the snake did not appear in the least distracted, while the curiosity of most of the birds should soon have been satisfied; the birds were making a remarkable fuss if they were merely the prey of conflicting emotions. While it may have been advantageous for them to point out that snakes eat fledglings, this hardly required a racket that attracted my attention several hundred metres away. Usually, when birds express anxiety, they tend to use softer, more ventriloquial notes which render their authors hard to locate (Marler 1957). It seems likely that the outcry under discussion, like that of a captive, was made with the deliberate purpose of attracting a second predator capable of putting an end to the first predator's activities. It seems possible that the discordant bird-calls used by hunters may sometimes also act in the same way, attracting either birds anxious to join in a mobbing, or predators in search of its object.

W. R. P. BOURNE
3 Contlaw Place, Milltimber, Aberdeen

When danger is close at hand, the defensive behaviour becomes more vigorous.

Defence behaviour of a flock of Coot.—There are some references in *The Handbook* to the behaviour of flocks of Coot (*Fulica atra*) when attacked by birds of prey. On 11th January 1953, at Cannock Reservoir, Staffordshire, I witnessed the same behaviour when a Herring Gull (*Larus argentatus*) dived over a scattered flock of about 300 Coot. Those on the fringe of the flock flew a few yards low over the water, with much splashing, towards the centre, so that the birds formed a compact circular patch. After another swoop the Herring Gull flew off and the birds in the flock then gradually drifted apart to become once more a straggling group.

The throwing up of water which is referred to in *The Handbook* as an "active communal defence" appeared in this instance to be merely a consequence of the hurried flight of the outermost birds. As the birds never had to rise much above the water, the feet and wings automatically caused the splashing.   J. LORD

Several times at Bharatpur in India I have seen similar behaviour from Coot and Red-crested Pochard flocks threatened by Marsh Harriers, but in each case after some minutes of 'harrying' the flock to and fro, the

Marsh Harrier struck successfully, seizing its prey from the tail-end of the moving flock and holding it submerged for some minutes to drown it before eating.

Professor Tinbergen illustrates another ploy, in this case successful.

Bullfinch escaping from cat by "playing dead".—On 23rd March 1958 I saw our cat coming down the lawn of our garden in Oxford, carrying a small bird in its mouth. It dropped it and began to "play" with it, alternately touching it tentatively with its front paw and, when it moved, quickly taking it in its mouth again. The prey was a male Bullfinch (*Pyrrhula pyrrhula*). The bird fluttered weakly at first and then, after a while, lay completely motionless on its back. The cat gave it two more hesitant pushes with its paw. When the bird did not move the cat started turning away. Just at that moment the bird suddenly flew off. The cat made a quick, grabbing movement after it, but missed it. The Bullfinch flew off in a straight line, landing approximately fifteen yards away in a bush, about ten feet above the ground. The cat did not follow.

This observation strongly suggested that it was the Bullfinch's "playing dead" which made the cat lose interest and which, therefore, may well have saved its life. It would be interesting to know how wild predators would respond in such situations because, if some were even occasionally distracted, this behaviour, which is found in so many small birds, would have definite survival value.

N. TINBERGEN

We should expect Peregrines, by their name and noble stature, to show aggression – as indeed they do, in circumstances ranging from attacks on dogs and humans to terrorising unfortunate fellow-raptors seeking safety on migration by choosing the shortest possible sea crossing of the Mediterranean at Gibraltar.

AGGRESSIVE BEHAVIOUR OF PEREGRINE.

JUST before the war I was in a garden near the Dorset coast and heard a loud screaming of hawks just over the brow of a grass field about a hundred yards away. I hurried to see what was happening, but a Fox Terrier and a Golden Labrador joined in the excitement and made better pace than I could up the hill.

When I came to the brow of the hill I saw an extraordinary sight. Two Peregrines (*Falco p. peregrinus*) had been fighting on the ground, and had reached such a state of exhaustion that they were barely able to fly. One flapped off along the ground pursued by the Labrador and reached safety in the hedge of a wood. The other, a falcon, stood her ground, grabbed the terrier by the nose and pinned him to the ground. The terrier was a strong dog, rather given to fighting and afraid of nothing. However, the falcon's attack completely baffled him and he remained motionless, clapped to the ground like a hare in its form, trying to look at me out of the tail of his eye for help or advice.

I knelt down, opened the Peregrine's grip and tucked the dog under my arm, as I wanted neither of them to hurt the other. The falcon with crown feathers erected and wings half expanded was a magnificent sight and I watched her at my feet for several minutes until she recovered her breath sufficiently to flutter along the grass, and gradually gaining height, made off for the cliff nearby.

Sham fights between Peregrines and Ravens are of almost daily occurrence here in the summer, but I have never before seen Peregrines fighting on the ground or with such ferocity, nor should I have expected one to tackle a dog three or four times her weight with such promptitude and success.   RALPH BOND.

PEREGRINE FALCON
ATTACKING A WOMAN.

AT the end of April 1922 a woman living near Yealmpton, Devon, seeing a large hawk attacking, as she thought, one of her fowls, went to the rescue. The hawk, instead of flying off, turned on her, tore her apron, and finally fixed its claws so firmly in her dress that it was unable to extricate them, and had to be killed. The bird proved to be a Peregrine (*Falco p. peregrinus*) and its victim not a fowl but a Kestrel (*F. t. tinnunculus*). Both birds are now in the possession of my brother, and are being set up by Mr. Chalkley, taxidermist, of Winchester. I would be very glad to know if such behaviour is common on the part of Peregrines or similar hawks. The Kestrel would seem to be an odd prey for a hawk of a different species.   P. E. A. MORSHEAD.

[Mr. John Yonge, of Puslinch, Yealmpton, has kindly forwarded the following more detailed account: " The incident occurred on April 28th, 1922. Mrs. Furzland, a woman aged about seventy, lives in a cottage near Puslinch Bridge on the river Yealm. She saw a large hawk on the ground apparently eating another bird, and thinking its prey was one of her chickens, she went to the rescue and tried to drive it away. When she got near, it flew at her, and clawed her apron and finally got its claws so firmly fixed in the stuff that she could not shake it off. She was somewhat frightened, thinking it would attack her face, so called to her grandson (a small boy), to bring his grandfather's walking stick, and with this weapon she killed the hawk. The bird it was mauling was a Kestrel. Whether it was really eating it I cannot say—but all the skin and flesh had been torn from the head—the rest of the body was uninjured. When Mrs. Furzland picked up the Kestrel it was dead and had only just been killed, but she did not actually see the Peregrine strike it down. She related the story to me herself, and I am quite sure there is no reason to doubt any part of it. She gave me the two birds and I sent them to Capt. R. Y. A. Morshead.   JOHN YONGE."

Persecution of migrating raptors by Peregrines at Gibraltar
Raptors migrating past Gibraltar are commonly attacked by locally-resident Peregrines *Falco peregrinus* of the small subspecies *brookei*, particularly during the northward passage, when the Peregrines are nesting. This causes a small but steady mortality among the migrants. Attacks are especially intense when directed against large raptors, the commonest of which is the Short-toed Eagle *Circaetus gallicus*. Usually, the repeated stoops by one or both of a Peregrine pair succeed in driving off the intruder.

In most cases of mobbing, physical contact does not occur; typically, an attacked raptor attempts to evade the stooping Peregrine by performing a half-roll or by suddenly changing its direction of flight. Nevertheless, physical contact is not infrequent and it must occasionally have the effect of stunning or injuring the migrant, since, although I have not seen a Peregrine actually strike down another raptor, I have seen marks on the head of a dead Short-toed Eagle which suggested that this is what had happened. Numerous eye-witnesses speak of raptors literally falling out of the sky after receiving blows from Peregrines. The more ferocious attacks occur over the east side of the Rock, where the eyrie of one Peregrine pair is situated. The coastal strip is narrow there, so that stunned raptors generally fall into the sea and drown, unless rescued (usually by inhabitants of nearby Catalan Bay village). The numbers affected vary from year to year: J. Saez of the village, who has been responsible for numerous rescues, has informed me that about six are

obtained alive from the sea annually. These usually recover quickly and are released in a safe locality. Presumably, an unknown but probably fairly small number does drown unnoticed. Short-toed Eagles account for most victims, but Booted Eagles *Hieraaetus pennatus* are also commonly rescued, as well as occasional Black Kites *Milvus migrans*, Griffon Vultures *Gyps fulvus* and, once, a female Sparrowhawk *Accipiter nisus*. On the other hand, the locally-commonest migrant raptor, the Honey Buzzard *Pernis apivorus*, appears to pass unscathed.

Passing raptors are also mobbed by Herring Gulls *Larus argentatus*, which often force them to land but have never been seen to make contact. Mobbing by large numbers of gulls may, however, bewilder raptors, which are then less able to evade stoops from the Peregrines.

E. F. J. GARCIA
50 Governor's Street, Gibraltar

Owls, too, have something of a reputation for aggression, and although (as the note suggests) a nest is unlikely so early in the year, Tawny Owls would certainly be defending breeding territories in January.

Tawny Owl attacking Fox in winter.—At 3.30 p.m. on 7th January 1964 I was watching a dog Fox *Vulpes vulpes* drinking at a pond near Risby, Yorkshire, when, without any warning, a Tawny Owl *Strix aluco* suddenly swooped down and attacked it. So far as I could see, the owl did not actually hold on to the Fox, but rather hovered over it and raked it about the head with its claws, all the time uttering a high-pitched, vibrant *kree-ee*. The immediate reaction of the Fox was to hug the earth and this it did for about ten seconds before running away across the open field (instead of along the hedgerow as might have been expected). The owl followed, still screaming and diving at it. At no time did the Fox offer any resistance.

Although I have heard of Tawny Owls attacking cats at night, a dog Fox is rather larger and the happenings described above took place in reasonably good light. The attack was entirely unprovoked and it seems highly unlikely that the owl would have had a nest in January. ANDREW PATERSON

Long-eared Owls attacking Foxes, Hare and man The behaviour of roosting Long-eared Owls *Asio otus* observed in West Germany by Wing Commander T. R. Holland (*Brit. Birds*, 67: 212-213) made interesting reading. Wing Commander Holland was most fortunate to locate a winter roost of approximateiy 50 owls; winter roosts in Britain rarely number more than 20 birds. I have made a field study of the Long-eared Owl for over 27 years, and have several records of aggressive behaviour towards large mammals.

On the very cold night of 21st February 1968, I was sitting under pines in one of the Forestry Commission's properties in Lincolnshire listening to a male and a female Long-eared Owl. At about 10.00 p.m. it began to snow and the owls stopped calling. It snowed for an hour, then the sky cleared slightly and the male began calling again. At 11.10 he flew above the ride close to where I was sitting, then turned, flew back and alighted in a tree about 15 metres from me. He resumed calling, so it was obvious that he was marking his territory. At 11.50 he vacated his perch and began to fly round and round just above the tops of the conifers, wing-clapping once every short circuit. At first I thought that this routine was part of his display flight, but then he turned rapidly and came in low above the snow-covered ride. There was an animal on the ride walking towards me, and when it was approximately 30 metres away I saw that it was a Fox *Vulpes vulpes*. The Long-eared Owl silently approached it from behind, about two metres above the ride. With feet extended downwards the owl swooped, causing the Fox to crouch. No contact was made. The owl turned along the ride and swooped again, and the Fox ran into cover almost opposite me.

In May 1968, while photographing Long-eared Owls in Nottinghamshire, I saw one of the adults swoop and scatter a trio of small Fox cubs which were exploring the ground close to my pylon hide. Similar behaviour was exacted upon an adult Fox in the same place one week later by the female owl. This display was accompanied by her vocal disapproval—an almost continuous 'whick-whack'.

In the early evening of 17th April 1970, my wife and I watched a hunting Long-eared Owl quartering a grass field about 300 metres from where its mate was brooding small young. The owl was quartering the field in strips, flying two or three metres above the ground. The flight was slow but deliberate, four to six wing-beats being followed by a glide, the latter occasionally punctuated by brief hovering (also observed by Wing Commander Holland, but seldom mentioned in the literature). For about five minutes the owl hunted unsuccessfully, then a Hare *Lepus europaeus* broke cover and ran diagonally across the field, pursued by the owl. Several times the Hare changed direction, and each time the owl cut across its line. Once, when the Hare stopped, the owl hovered just above it with legs down and claws extended, but no direct contact was made. For ten minutes the game continued; eventually the owl turned away to continue the more serious business of hunting animals within its prey range.

I have only once encounted a Long-eared Owl which assaulted human beings, and that was a female at a Lincolnshire site in 1961. Her repeated attacks were made only after her young were 16 to 17 days old. She flew at me on eight separate occasions, striking me twice, once with her feet and once with her claws. She also attacked two other observers, Douglas Atkinson and John Richards, drawing blood on the former's head and twice assaulting the latter, lacerating his left ear. A. C. Bent, in *Life Histories of North American Birds of Prey* (vol. 2, 1938), mentioned that a Mr Joseph Dixon was attacked several times by a Long-eared Owl while he was attempting to photograph her young. At first she used only her wings, but later she struck with her claws, and once inflicted slight wounds in his scalp.

DERICK SCOTT

West View, Walkeringham, Doncaster, South Yorkshire DN10 4HZ

Although lacking beak or talons to back up its threats, one sea-bird, the Fulmar, is well able to defend itself. Most bird watchers who venture into or near a Fulmar colony are attacked by the sitting birds and liberally spattered with a particularly foul-smelling and persistent oil that penetrates clothing and hangs about for years as a reminder of the experience – one shared by these sheep.

Sheep contaminated by Fulmar oil During the autumn of 1972, on Fetlar, Shetland, a crofter showed me several sheep that had been contaminated by oil from Fulmars *Fulmarus glacialis*. The wool was matted and sticky, with particles of heather, grass and other materials adhering to it; in severe cases the wool had formed a black, sticky lump. The crofter considered that he would be unable to sell sheep in that condition and, of course, the fleeces were useless.

In the area where these particular sheep were kept there was an 'inland' colony of Fulmars. About 14 pairs nested on a rocky outcrop about 500 metres from the sea. It appears that the feeding sheep had strayed too close to the nesting Fulmars and had received the usual treatment meted out to intruders. From the extent of the oiling, sometimes on both sides of the animal, it seems that the sheep had been repeatedly oiled, and that they had not been alarmed or discouraged by the initial contact with the Fulmars but had continued to feed within range of the sitting birds.

With the rapidly increasing population of Fulmars, more and more inland sites are being used and this hazard to sheep seems likely to increase. Understandably the Fulmar is fast becoming an unpopular bird among the crofters.

IAIN S. ROBERTSON
Portland Bird Observatory and Field Centre, Old Lower Light, Portland, Dorset

Aerial bombardment is less usual but, as shown in this note from Shetland, very effective.

FULMAR EJECTING OIL IN DELIBERATE ATTACK.

IN July, 1943, I was climbing casually up a cliff at the Knab, Lerwick, Shetland, when I approached a sitting Fulmar (*Fulmarus g. glacialis*) from below. The bird was on a fairly wide ledge; we were both surprised and the Fulmar left the nest and flew away immediately without any demonstration. As I climbed upwards past the nest a fair quantity of oil splashed on to the rock slightly above my right shoulder and I turned carefully around to see the bird in orbit before returning to the attack, this time a "dry run". The swoops, which brought the bird to within two yards of my head, were repeated some half-dozen times, and my companion, who was two or three yards below me,

reported that the ejaculation was made at a similar distance, the oil having the added momentum given by the swoop.

There was no doubt about the deliberateness of the attack and the view that the ejaculation is a defensive reflex could not be held true in this case. The egg was practically fresh.

Subsequent enquiry, on Fair Isle among other places, has elicited no account of similar behaviour in the species.

ALFRED HAZELWOOD.

On St Kilda some years ago I saw a Fulmar jump off its nest (with great ease, so strong was the updraught on the 1000-foot cliff-face) and swoop, 'spitting' furiously at a passing Raven. This unfortunate bird promptly landed and preened itself vigorously in an attempt to keep its plumage in some sort of condition, so it seems very likely that these observations from Orkney are the results of aerial attack.

Peregrine and Raven possibly contaminated by Fulmar oil
With reference to R. A. Broad's paper on Fulmar *Fulmarus glacialis* oil contamination (*Brit. Birds*, 67: 297-301), the following observations of possible oiling may be of interest. On 10th June 1971, I disturbed a female Peregrine *Falco peregrinus* from a low cliff near Waulkmill Bay, Orkney. The bird's plumage appeared very wet and bedraggled as though the feathers were saturated with some substance. It flew away with some difficulty across the bay. On 14th May 1973, at Backaskaill, Sanday, Orkney, I came upon a Raven *Corvus corax* resting under a bank. Again, the feathers appeared saturated and stuck together. As it flew away it managed to rise only a metre or two above the ground. Both these birds allowed much closer approach than is usual and I do not think they would have survived for very long. On neither occasion had it been raining and there were no pools suitable for bathing. Fulmars were plentiful on the cliffs near both areas, however, and it is highly likely that the state of the plumage of the Peregrine and the Raven was due to contamination by Fulmar oil.   C. J BOOTH

34 High Street, Kirkwall, Orkney KW15 1AZ

Another display of aggression shows considerable pluck in an unexpected species.

Ring Ouzels attacking Adder at their nest.—On 24th July 1963 I was walking over moorland near Wooler, Northumberland, when I saw a Ring Ouzel *Turdus torquatus* acting rather strangely. It kept flying over to a patch of grass about six feet square and then diving like a hawk, all the time uttering an unusual call. I sat down on a rock about fifty yards away and watched this behaviour for a quarter of an hour. Eventually the bird was joined by another Ring Ouzel and then a Curlew *Numenius arquata*, so to satisfy my curiosity I walked down to the patch of grass and there found a large Adder *Vipera berus* curled up on top of a tussock. I killed it with a stick and then found the Ring Ouzels' nest about three feet from it. This contained one egg which was quite intact except for two small holes in the shell. There were also fragments of egg-shell where the Adder had been lying and I assumed that it had destroyed the clutch.   JOHN ANDERSON

Yet another is fascinating in provoking speculation on both the evolution *and* the likely success of the technique involved.

Threat display of Green Woodpecker.—On 11th January 1955 at 4.15 p.m. at The Lee, Gt. Missenden, Buckinghamshire, a Green Woodpecker (*Picus viridis*) flew up from the ground on to an ash tree often used for nesting. I was standing at a gate near-by, and when the bird noticed me it flew on to the nearest branch (about 20 yards away) and proceeded to swing its head, neck and body from side to side in a regular pendulum-like motion, lowering its head in the middle of each swing. As it moved its head it stared, or rather glared, with the left eye and then the right eye, alternately, and when staring uttered three calls—"ha-ha-ha." This occurred seven or eight times, then the bird flew to below an old nesting-hole and went to roost.

This appears to be a threat-display, but also very much resembles that described by D. W. Snow and A. W. G. Manning in their account of courtship-display (*antea*, vol. xlvii, p. 355).

SUSAN COWDY

Those of us who have experienced walking through a Great Skua colony, with infuriated parents diving out of the sun at our heads, often from two angles at once, certainly remember the frequent, and painful, clip of a wing across the head and the noise of the rush of air as, dive-bomber like, the Skuas pull out of their dive only inches away. Thus we can imagine how intruders into a Lapwing territory may feel intimidated, especially as the rounded, fingered wings of the Lapwing seem ideally shaped to produce maximum noise.

Lapwing's persistent attack on Fox.—At 4.55 a.m. on 13th May 1962 I was travelling along a road near Deene, which is about five miles from Corby, Northamptonshire, when I saw a Fox (*Vulpes vulpes*) picking its way through a narrow belt of trees and I stopped to watch. Carefully stalking into the open, it suddenly pounced and from almost between its feet arose a Lapwing (*Vanellus vanellus*). The bird, which presumably had a nest or young in the vicinity, flew over the Fox and began to dive at it in a most determined fashion. The attack was pressed home with great vigour and the Fox slowly retreated, snapping at the bird as it did so. This went on for some fifty or sixty yards before the Fox turned and loped away across the parkland. Although I have often watched Lapwings attack other birds, this is the first time I have seen one go for a mammal and it was its persistence which surprised me.

N. L. Hodson

LAPWING DRIVING SHEEP FROM NEST.

Whilst in Sutherlandshire in May, 1936, I saw a Lapwing (*Vanellus vanellus*) continually jumping on to the back of a sheep and pecking at it in an effort to drive the sheep from the nesting site. Whilst on the ground the bird followed the sheep around, keeping in front of its face with wide open wings. The vacant look of surprise on the face of the sheep was amusing to see.

G. E. Took.

The discomfiture caused even to innocent bystanders by the vehemence of these attacks is often clearly apparent. Some years ago, in Norfolk, I watched a pair of Grey Partridges wander, quite aimlessly and with no malice aforethought, down the furrows of a ploughed field right into a Lapwing territory. The wrath of the Lapwings was inevitably unleashed, and the poor Partridges fled the attack as best they could, the male trying to preserve the vestiges of dignity by turning and standing tall to face the dive-bombers on each sortie, ducking only at the last minute.

Obviously such displays often succeed in their prime purpose. Such aggression, sometimes physically painful, must, at the very least, be most distracting to the intruder. It is not difficult to imagine that the concentration that a predator needs to make a successful find of nest or young would very quickly be disturbed.

Index

—— Index of Authors ——